Autism and Eating Disorders in Teens

by the same author

Working with Girls and Young Women with an
Autism Spectrum Condition
A Practical Guide for Clinicians
Fiona Fisher Bullivant
ISBN 978 1 78592 420 0
eISBN 978 1 78450 784 8

of related interest

Food Refusal and Avoidant Eating in Children,
including those with Autism Spectrum Conditions
A Practical Guide for Parents and Professionals
Gillian Harris and Elizabeth Shea
ISBN 978 1 78592 318 0
eISBN 978 1 78450 632 2

A Guide to Mental Health Issues in Girls and
Young Women on the Autism Spectrum
Diagnosis, Intervention and Family Support
Dr Judy Eaton
ISBN 978 1 78592 092 9
eISBN 978 1 78450 355 0

A Short Introduction to Understanding and Supporting
Children and Young People with Eating Disorders
Lucy Watson and Bryan Lask
ISBN 978 1 84905 627 4
eISBN 978 1 78450 102 0

Self-Harm and Eating Disorders in Schools
A Guide to Whole-School Strategies and Practical Support
Pooky Knightsmith
ISBN 978 1 84905 584 0
eISBN 978 1 78450 031 3

Can I tell you about Eating Disorders?
A guide for friends, family and professionals
Bryan Lask and Lucy Watson
ISBN 978 1 84905 421 8
eISBN 978 0 85700 797 1

Autism and Eating Disorders in Teens

A Guide for Parents and Professionals

FIONA FISHER BULLIVANT
and SHARLEEN WOODS

Jessica Kingsley Publishers
London and Philadelphia

First published in Great Britain in 2020 by Jessica Kingsley Publishers

An Hachette Company

1

A CIP catalogue record for this title is available from the
British Library and the Library of Congress

ISBN 978 1 78775 292 4
eISBN 978 1 7877 5293 1

Printed and bound by CPI Group (UK) Ltd, Croydon, CR0 4YY

Jessica Kingsley Publishers' policy is to use papers that are natural,
renewable and recyclable products and made from wood grown in
sustainable forests. The logging and manufacturing processes are expected
to conform to the environmental regulations of the country of origin.

Jessica Kingsley Publishers
73 Collier Street
London N1 9BE, UK

www.jkp.com

Sharleen: To my mum and dad, Marguerite and Stewart, for your unwavering love, support and belief in me as a person and what I can achieve.

Fiona: To my parents, Mavis and Michael Fisher. Thank you for your unconditional love and support and for introducing the outdoors into my life at such an early age, so that I learnt to appreciate and love the mountains, the sea, lakes, rivers and seasons.

Contents

People think autism is a bad thing, but being diagnosed with autism helped me realize that I'm not the problem. I'm not just weird anymore. It's not my fault if I can't quite fit in. That gave me the confidence I needed to be excited about life again because now I know it's ok to be a little quirky. That's what anorexic me needed to hear.

(Niamh)

Preface

Each and every one of us has a relationship with food. A relationship that has been shaped and influenced by multiple factors – biology, family, culture, availability, environment; to name but a few. For some, complexity arises when this relationship starts to negatively impact on daily functioning, impairing both mental and physical health to debilitating levels. In the clinical world of eating disorders there are, indeed, similarities, as there are familiar differences in presentation and individual experience. However, difficulty arises in engagement when the not-so-frequent 'unfamiliar' or subtle differences are overlooked or even misunderstood by the systems around a young person. This results in clinicians finding themselves in challenging and different positions on how to effectively support such young people.

This book is the result of recurring 'corridor conversations' and consultations across our respective roles and teams, where we – Fiona, an autism learning disability specialist nurse within Child and Adolescent Mental Health Services (CAMHS), and Sharleen, an advanced dietitian within Children and Young People Community Eating Disorder Services (CYP CEDS) – began to notice these subtle but pivotal 'differences' in an effort to meet the needs of the young people we were working with.

These 'differences' or autistic traits have been explored by Baron-Cohen, Leslie and Frith (1985), Davies *et al.* (2011), Russell *et al.* (2009) and Tchanturia, Happe and Godley (2004). Most people think of autism and eating disorders as being completely different

9

conditions. However, these researchers have identified traits that are similar to both autism and eating disorders, that is, difficulties with:

- flexible thinking

- theory of mind

- emotional processing

- emotional literacy.

As girls with autism are frequently underdiagnosed, it's often an eating disorder that first brings them to clinical attention. Although men and boys with autism can and do develop eating disorders, most of the research and clinical focus on autism and eating disorders has been on girls and women. This gender bias has led the media to coin the term 'female Asperger's' for the eating disorder anorexia nervosa (*The Times* 2007). A small study in 2017 found that 23% of women hospitalized for anorexia met the diagnostic criteria for autism (Westwood, Mandy and Tchanturia 2017), with further research indicating that the aforementioned underlying traits preceded the onset of the disorder (Mette Bentz *et al.* 2017; Schulte-Ruther *et al.* 2012).

Significantly heightened autistic traits in people with anorexia nervosa are correlated with more severe presentations and poorer outcomes (Nielsen *et al.* 2015; Tchanturia, Larsson and Adamson 2016; Tchanturia *et al.* 2017), leading to indications that traditional therapeutic methods may need to be altered for this cohort (Treasure 2013). Indeed, the literature also cites difficulties encountered by clinicians in managing individuals with autism and eating disorders, with intervention largely being based on individual practitioner experience (Kinnaird, Norton and Tchanturia 2017).

SO, WHO ARE WE?

We are passionate and experienced clinicians who place young people at the heart of what we do. We proactively challenge current ways of thinking whilst exploring and identifying what needs to change. We have observed an often missed or misinterpreted link between eating disorders and autism, and we hope that by sharing our ideas and findings with a wider audience, we will scaffold the need for change and a move towards a more integrated service for young people with eating disorders and autism.

Fiona

My background is 33 years as a practitioner in the field of autism and learning disabilities, and more recently attention deficit hyperactivity disorder (ADHD) and eating disorders within children's community, CAMHS, residential settings, and special/alternative and mainstream schools. I will largely be discussing the perspective of autism within the context of this book.

I found myself being approached more and more by clinicians from the eating disorders service (in particular, Sharleen), whose young patients:

- were not responding to treatment within their team

- did not fit a classical eating disorder profile

- had a difference about the way they were interacting and communicating and/or describing/expressing their eating disorder.

From some initial joint working it became apparent that if the clinicians used different means and types of assessment and questioning, and moved away from a traditional model of care, positive shifts in the clinical presentation of the young people started to emerge.

Sharleen

I have been working in the field of nutrition for over ten years, mostly as a community-based dietitian in the field of paediatrics and mental health, where I regularly encounter children with autism and significant eating difficulties (extreme food aversions and enteral [artificial] feeding). I entered the clinical realm of eating disorders by chance in 2015, and although it is challenging, I have never looked back. I will mainly be discussing the perspective of eating disorders within the context of this book.

Increasingly, I noticed that a number of young people in my caseload were presenting 'differently' and that standard approaches of intervention were not working within both my own and my colleagues' sessions. As a result, I and others on my team sought alternative ways of working and thinking, and we approached Fiona to help us develop and adjust our practice to meet our young people's needs. Fiona's effective words 'enter their world' developed the foundations of our collaborative working relationship and a 'one size does not fit all' approach.

* * *

This book is the result of a 'meeting of our two minds', exploring autism in the context of eating disorders. We discuss sensory issues and the relationship with avoidant restrictive food intake disorder (ARFID), as well as co-morbidities which often get missed or overlooked by rigid clinical pathways and ways of thinking. We describe and analyse the current pathways within CAMHS and CYP CEDS in relation to the identification and assessment of autism/ eating disorders as well as interventions and treatments, exploring our individual and collaborative experiences of young people and services. Through the use of case studies to highlight what didn't work well, what did work well, and what needed to be different for those individuals, we scaffold the need for change in clinical practice and demonstrate the importance of confident and flexible multi-disciplinary working for early identification and assessment, clinically sound formulation, and evidence-based therapeutic interventions that are not only person-centred but family- and system-focused. This approach will ensure that young people with autism and eating disorders will have every opportunity to reach their potential for emotional and physical well-being.

We sincerely believe that our book is a timely resource that will support our colleagues and clinicians working in this field.

Acknowledgements

We would like to thank our friends and family for supporting us throughout our book journey.

Thanks also to our teachers at primary school who made it such a wonderfully nurturing, caring, inspiring, learning experience: Mrs Patterson, Mrs Charnley, Mrs Isabelle Robinson, Mrs Redmayne; and Mr Frank Stec, Mrs Irene Thornhill and Mr O'Neill, who led the school.

We would like to acknowledge those clinicians we have worked with and still work with, who put in long hours and sacrifice time that could be spent with their own families in order to ensure that the children and young people they work with get the best-quality service possible. Their dedication and knowledge flow throughout this book as much as ours.

We would like to thank all the young people and their families whom we have met and continue to meet on their journeys. Thank you for letting us sit alongside you when you are at your most vulnerable. Your courage and strength inspire us every day.

Last, but not least, we wish to thank our contributors.

Most importantly, thank you to Niamh, an extraordinary young woman who has shown such resilience and a motivation to understand herself. It is because of Niamh that the idea for this book came about. Niamh, you are an inspiration and we are honoured to know you.

We would like to thank Niamh's mum, Mandy, for her honest and moving reflections about her and her daughter's experiences of autism and eating disorder.

We would like to thank Jake Price and his mum, Samantha, for their contribution. We are immensely proud of how far you have come and your bravery in sharing your story.

Thank you to Kay and Ruth for sharing your ongoing journeys. Your reflections and insight will influence future direction for those with autism and eating disorders.

Thank you to Samuel Coppard, a senior family therapist currently working in CYP CEDS, for his contribution. We have learned so much from Sam – not only in terms of supervision but because of his willingness to adapt his practice to the young people and the families in front of him. It is therapists like Sam who will shape future therapeutic practice.

Thank you to Emilie Daniels, who continues to not only stretch and improve her own clinical skills but goes the extra mile to find different ways of working in order to connect with the young people she encounters and their families.

Thank you to the other health care practitioners who contributed to this book.

Notes on the Text

Throughout this book we use the terms 'autism', 'ASC' (autism spectrum condition) and 'ASD' (autism spectrum disorder) as the book's content spans some 10+ years in which the terminology has changed. In order to respect the individuals who have kindly agreed to share their story, we have included the diagnostic terminology in the way that it was given to them at that time.

Heidi is an anonymized case study; therefore, aspects of her care have been changed in order to preserve her anonymity.

'Think Differently'

Introduction

In recent years there has been a lot of media attention on autism and eating disorders, either occurring independently or together. However, despite this growing interest, there is still a lack of understanding not only among the general public but also among those working in the health and social care sectors. Individually, both conditions are highly intricate, requiring skilful identification, assessment and intervention within the clinical setting. This book will outline these processes and show how subtle yet complex differences are often overlooked but are imperative to take account of in the provision of care. As you read, you will notice common themes arising in the experience of services with autism and eating disorders.

SYSTEMIC EFFECT

It will soon become evident that the systems, whether education, health care or social care, don't understand the context of the problems faced by our young people, especially those with autism. In fact, we struggle to understand the nuances of autism. We either don't notice a difference – due to lack of experience, awareness and training – or we do but we do nothing because it doesn't fit in a recognized pathway or we don't know what to do with that clinical presentation. We often hear from schools that they do not have any concerns with these young people; they are academically bright, high achievers/performers and perfectionists, albeit 'shy', 'a bit unusual' and/or 'preferring adult company'. We are highly aware that our systems are not set up to manage the difference that autism and eating disorders brings, and our ability to offer multi-agency work is limited by the processes within and across each of these systems.

INDIVIDUAL IMPACT

In order to make a difference, we need to start as individual clinicians to change our practices – from assessment, formulation and risk management right through to therapy interventions and discharge – in order to meet the needs of the young person in front of us. This is required in all settings: inpatient and community. It only takes one person to cause the ripple effect that can change the outcome.

We know that practitioners are under huge pressure in terms of performance and time, because we are those practitioners working with these young people every day. That said, getting it right from the outset will undoubtedly help the pressures of the system downstream. For example, with early identification and intervention of the problem, we can reduce crisis management and inpatient admissions later. We also need to highlight differences in clinical presentations to senior leadership teams and to commissioners so that appropriate funding and training are implemented – it would be naïve to think that the influence of national agendas such as reducing obesity and the ever-revolving door of diet culture do not impact on those with obsessional and rigid tendencies. This cohort of people need to be accounted for when developing services.

THE IMPORTANCE OF THE YOUNG PERSON

Individual experiences are key. It is these stories that will inform practice and shift dynamics of research to address aspects such as effective therapy modalities, gender bias and defining eating disorder recovery to meet individual needs. Early on, this book provides an opportunity to practise reflection through case studies of young people and adults who wanted to share their stories with you (their words are also scattered throughout the book). We ask you to be curious as you read these case studies, so that you can dive deep into subsequent chapters which explore and analyse care provision for those with autism and eating disorders.

We unpick the intricacy that comes with autism and eating disorders and provide food for thought (no pun intended!) on how to work with these young people and their families.

THE STRUCTURE OF THE BOOK

Below is a brief summary of each chapter to guide you through the content of the book.

Chapter 1: Understanding Autism and Eating Disorders

Here we define and describe what eating disorders and autism are, independently of each other. We look at the difference between disordered eating and eating disorders as this is often an area where practitioners become stuck. We walk you through the ever-evolving landscape in autism terminology and how history has shaped our current understanding. This is followed by a brief description of current clinical pathways, the outcome measures utilized within services, and the numbers of people affected by each of these conditions, separately and collectively. By providing the underpinnings of these conditions individually, this chapter will prepare you for the remainder of the book, which analyses the web of complexity when eating disorders and autism present conjointly.

Chapter 2: Journeys and Reflections

As already indicated, we not only illustrate our findings through a clinical and professional lens, but we also capture the voices of those who have and continue to experience autism and eating disorders first-hand. In this chapter, we provide an overarching view of two young people's journeys (those of Niamh and Heidi) through services, from referral to discharge. Detailed descriptions are provided here in order to provoke your curiosity and enable reflection on your own practice, whether that is professional or personal. Niamh and her mum, Mandy, talk about their experiences in the hope that their story will help others. We also include reflections from adults who have a diagnosis of autism and who had, or continue to experience, an eating disorder. The voices of these young people and adults form the backbone of the book.

Chapter 3: Assessment

The assessment process is arguably one of the most important stages in a young person's mental health care, as this is what determines future care pathways. We describe current assessment processes for both eating disorders and autism individually. How information is obtained differs because the aims for each condition are perceived as completely separate. We introduce how facets from each discipline can be interwoven within the assessment process, with emphasis on contextualizing the problem.

Chapter 4: Identification and Formulation

Using both Niamh's and Heidi's journeys as examples, we share our personal reflections on identifying autism in practice and why it can often be missed or overlooked. We provide ideas on what is needed in order to be more confident about identification of autism and the possible clues that require further exploration to determine its presence or not. This leads us into defining and exploring the process of formulation with regard to our understanding of eating difficulties in the context of autism, once identified. You will then see how the identification of autism reshapes the formulation process and determines subsequent care.

Chapter 5: Co-morbidities, Considerations and Risk

Although the focus of this book is on autism and eating disorders, it is important to be acutely aware that other health considerations (both mental and physical) may also be present and at play. The focus of this chapter is not to cover all conditions but to highlight those that in our experience are most commonly seen in this cohort of young people. In addition, we cover the risk associated with such presentations as well as aspects that impact on how we work therapeutically with these young people. Often these aspects are not necessarily 'diagnosable' but have a significant impact on daily functioning; for example, sensory needs, environment, school provision and sleep.

Chapter 6: Therapy and Interventions

In this chapter, we explore evidence-based therapeutic approaches and interventions recommended to treat and manage each of these complex clinical areas. Through the voices of those who have lived experiences, we analyse what works, what doesn't work and what requires adaptation in order to meet the needs of those with eating disorders and autism. Nutritional strategies are also discussed, as well as the different environments where interventions occur and how this impacts 'recovery' with respect to the eating disorder in those with autism.

Chapter 7: Recovery and Understanding of Self

Mindful of the interpretation of recovery, we explore what renourishment looks like in the context of co-occurring autism and what it means for those who have experienced this. As practitioners working in each of the respective areas, we reflect on what recovery and understanding of self means to us and how this has adapted in order to meet the needs of the individual in front of us who has both conditions. We also explore labelling and diagnoses and the impact of this on young people's lives, as well as what it means for current and future care.

Chapter 8: Service and Culture Change

It is important to gain understanding on what needs to change at a system and individual level in order for people to identify and work with these young people. This chapter explores aspects such as access to treatment, training and education, as well as empowering professionals and research. These are aspects highlighted throughout the book by those with lived experiences. It can often feel like a

Herculean task to make a difference on an individual level that will significantly impact on a systemic level; however, we often have resources within our system that we do not access or are unaware of. We hope that this chapter, alongside the preceding ones, will evoke curiosity about what can be done differently.

* * *

If you have picked up this book, it is likely that you work in this clinical area or you have experienced first-hand the implications of having either autism or an eating disorder, or both autism and an eating disorder together. If so, we hope that you will find this book useful, our focus being to provide an insight into the lives of people who are affected and the systems around them. We hope that you can signpost this resource to others, such as school, health and social systems, and even family and friends, who may require a deeper understanding of the issues.

CHAPTER 1

Understanding Autism and Eating Disorders

Both eating disorders and autism are complex clinical areas independently, often requiring specialist provision in the identification, management and intervention of each. In order to navigate the intertwined complexity of co-occurring autism and eating disorders, we first need to understand both of them individually in terms of definitions, epidemiology, current service pathways and how we monitor progress.

EATING DISORDERS
Distinguishing between disordered eating and eating disorders

The difference between disordered eating and eating disorders can be confusing and frustrating – not only for the general public but also for health care clinicians – with each term being used interchangeably in the media and research literature. With the increasing influence of diet culture in current Westernized society, it is not surprising that there is a reported increase in people engaging in disordered eating at some point in their lifetime (Bould *et al.* 2018; Gauvin, Steiger and Brodeur 2008; Hay 1998; Neumark-Sztainer *et al.* 2011; Reba-Harreleson *et al.* 2009). These disordered behaviours often begin in childhood or adolescence and are precursors for developing clinically definable eating disorders; therefore it is important to distinguish between the two entities.

What is disordered eating?

Disordered eating is a descriptive term explaining eating behaviours that are of lower severity and frequency level than those that fit within the confines of an eating disorder diagnosis. For experienced clinicians who work in the field, the differing presentations can usually, but not always, be clearly identified. For those less familiar with the field, it can be useful to view the relationship with food, body image and eating as a continuum ranging from 'normal and healthy' through to eating disorders that severely impact daily functioning, with disordered eating somewhere between the two (Russell-Mayhew 2007). Indeed, even describing 'normal' and 'healthy' proves problematic as their definitions are also now interlaced with diet culture influences. In this instance, normal healthy eating is about having invested consideration to food selection that is nutritious but it does not exclude having food that is enjoyable.

Disordered eating can also be used to describe eating difficulties in the context of other mental and physical health difficulties. It is not unusual to see food restriction or even purging, for example, in those who are experiencing depression and/or anxiety. The context in which these difficulties arise is key in ensuring effective management and is also an important consideration in those with autism, a consideration that will be explored later in this book.

What are eating disorders?

By definition, eating disorders are an unhealthy relationship with food and weight that interferes with many areas of a person's life. They are complex medical and psychiatric illnesses that can have severe consequences for health, productivity and relationships. There is no single reason as to why someone develops an eating disorder. Eating disorders are bio-psycho-social diseases, which means that a number of factors, such as biological, genetic, psychological, environmental and social influences, need to combine to increase the likelihood that a person develops an eating disorder. Eating disorders are not a fad, phase or lifestyle choice.

The most common forms of eating disorders include 'anorexia nervosa', 'bulimia nervosa', 'binge-eating disorder' and 'other specified feeding and eating disorder'.

ANOREXIA NERVOSA (AN)

AN has the highest mortality rate of any psychiatric disorder. It is characterized by restricting food to the point where it leads to weight loss or a failure to gain weight that results in a significantly low body weight compared with what would be expected for someone's age, sex and height. It is important to highlight that this occurs because of an intense fear of gaining weight or becoming fat alongside the person having a distorted view of themselves and/or their condition. These eating disorder cognitions are what distinguish AN from other physical or mental health problems that can result in weight loss. Diagnostic criteria of AN include two sub-types of the disorder:

- *Restrictive:* This is the stereotypical illness where the individual primarily restricts food and may engage in excessive compulsive exercise. There is no binge-eating (i.e. eating excessively large amounts of food in a short period of time) or purging (i.e. self-induced vomiting or the misuse of laxatives, diuretics or weight-loss preparations).

- *Binge–purge:* Food restriction and/or excessive exercise still occur, but there is also regular engagement in binge-eating and/or purging behaviours.

BULIMIA NERVOSA (BN)

BN is characterized by eating a large amount of food in a short period of time (i.e. bingeing), followed by efforts to counteract the 'fattening' effects of these foods by means of one or more of the following: self-induced vomiting, use of drugs such as laxatives and/or diuretics (purging) and/or alternating periods of starvation. Like AN, there is also an intense fear of gaining weight; however, because of the repeated binge–purge cycle, weight is often normal, or at a higher range, and stable.

BINGE-EATING DISORDER (BED)

BED is characterized by regular consumption of large quantities of food in a short space of time (often very quickly and to the point of discomfort), accompanied by feelings of loss of control, guilt and shame. Unlike people with BN, those with BED do not use purging methods after a binge but will feel an overwhelming sense of guilt associated with their loss of control.

OTHER SPECIFIED FEEDING AND EATING DISORDER (OSFED)
OSFED was previously known as 'eating disorder, not otherwise specified' (EDNOS); however, the latter term is no longer used. OSFED is used to describe eating disorders that do not meet all the diagnostic criteria for the aforementioned eating disorders, but the people still have maladaptive thoughts and behaviours related to food, eating and body image. These include:

- Atypical anorexia nervosa: meeting all of the symptoms of typical AN, except that weight is at or above normal range.

- Bulimia nervosa of low frequency and/or limited duration.

- Binge-eating disorder of low frequency and/or limited duration.

- Purging disorder: purging, only without any bingeing episodes.

- Night eating syndrome: consuming at least a quarter of daily intake after the evening meal. Waking up after going to bed in order to eat may also occur.

National guidelines and diagnostic criteria

The National Institute of Health and Care Excellence (NICE) guidelines recommend the evidence-based treatment of AN, BN, BED and OSFED (NICE 2017). It is these recommendations that provide the framework to eating disorder service provision nationwide.

However, adhering to this framework has been problematic because of the clinical categorization of eating disorders being changed in the most recently published *Diagnostic and Statistical Manual of Psychiatric Disorders* (*DSM-5*; American Psychiatric Association 2013) and the latest *International Classification of Diseases* (*ICD-11*; World Health Organization 2018). The previously termed 'feeding disorders' are now grouped with eating disorders under the category of 'feeding and eating disorders', including the following:

- *ARFID:* Previously referred to as 'selective eating disorder', ARFID is characterized by a persistent food restriction where nutritional needs are not met, resulting in deficiencies and/or significant weight loss. Food restriction occurs due to a loss of interest in food, concerns about the consequences of eating (e.g. vomiting) and/or avoidance due to the sensory characteristics of food. Unlike AN and BN, there are no weight or shape concerns and it often, but not always, co-occurs with ASC.

- *Pica:* This is the persistent eating of non-food items that have no nutritional value (e.g. dirt, paper, paint, etc.).

- *Rumination disorder:* Repetitive, habitual bringing up of food that might be partly digested. Regurgitated food may be re-chewed, re-swallowed or spat out.

ARFID, pica and rumination disorder are not included in NICE guidelines. This has caused difficulties with regard to suitable service access and provision, especially as ARFID can be co-occurring in presentations of autism.

'Orthorexia' and 'obesity'

Controversially, neither 'orthorexia' nor 'obesity' are classified as eating disorders. Orthorexia is a term used to describe obsessive behaviours in the pursuit of a 'healthy' diet. Obesity is a clinical definition for people of higher weight who meet classifications defined by a weight metric rather than thoughts and behaviours. An aspect often overlooked is that those with larger bodies may also have an eating disorder and therefore weight should not be used in isolation when determining the presence of an eating disorder. Needless to say, both 'orthorexia' and 'obesity' are risk factors to developing eating disorders.

Epidemiology of eating disorders

Determining the incidence and prevalence of eating disorders is challenging. Although there have been some well-designed studies, there has not been any robust scientific research from which to draw conclusions. Factors such as the ever-changing and differing landscape of diagnostic criteria, as well as variability in data collection (often reserved to inpatient settings and not accounting for private treatment), contribute to the difficulty (Currin *et al.* 2005; Field *et al.* 2012; Keski-Rahkonen *et al.* 2007; Van Son *et al.* 2006). Indeed, the very nature of eating disorders (secrecy and denial by those who are suffering from them) suggests that there are also significant numbers of people who are undiagnosed/undetected, who will not be captured in any national data (Solmi *et al.* 2016).

It is estimated that 1.6 million people in the United Kingdom have an eating disorder (BEAT 2015). It is not known exactly what percentage of this figure is the current adolescent population; however, the evidence does suggest that most eating disorders originate in the adolescent years (Fairburn and Harrison 2003; Machado *et al.* 2007). The majority of the data stems from research when classification was based on *DSM-IV* (American Psychiatric Association 2000), where the previously termed EDNOS was the most prevalent eating disorder, accounting for 2% to 5% of the general population (Fairburn and Bohn 2005; Machado *et al.* 2007; Smink, van Hoeken and Hoek 2012), whilst lifetime prevalence of AN was estimated to range between 0.3% and 0.9%, for BN it was between 0.9% and 1.5% and for BED between 1.9% and 3.5% (Micali *et al.* 2013; Smink *et al.* 2012). Eating disorders have the highest mortality rate amongst all psychiatric illnesses (Arcelus *et al.* 2011).

Men and ethnic minorities

Little is known about the manifestation and epidemiology of eating disorders in men and in ethnic minorities, the majority of research being from samples of European or North American white females. There is an approximation that between 10% and 25% of the eating disorder population is male, with an observed increased in men accessing eating disorder treatment (Sweeting *et al.* 2015).

Eating disorders – current pathway

In 2015, NHS England published access and waiting time standards for children and young people with a suspected eating disorder, providing assessment and NICE-concordant intervention within four weeks for routine presentations, within one week for urgent presentations and within 24 hours for emergency presentations (NHS England 2015). Frustratingly, there are no directives within these standards on what determines the difference between routine, urgent and emergency, and therefore this is led by each individual service. From a personal perspective, urgent and emergency cases are often determined due to physical health risk such as low body weight, physical health symptomology, and/or rapid and significant weight loss. This can often mean that specialist eating disorder teams are crisis managing children and young people who are indeed at risk of physical health consequences due to starvation but who do not meet the criteria for an eating disorder. This proves an ethical dilemma for such services where there is often no service to meet the alternative need. Indeed, this is often what transpires when a child or young person presents with autism and significant eating difficulties. We will discuss this in more depth throughout the course of the book.

Alongside the publication of the standards, additional funding was provided by the government to establish specialist service provision in order to meet the standards by 2020. Unfortunately, this funding was not stipulated to be ring-fenced and therefore the type of provision still remains variable throughout the United Kingdom. At present, the majority of referrals enter the system via the traditional route of the general practitioner (GP) or via a school professional, with self-referral being recommended as an embedded criterion for point of entry in the future. For self-referral to be effective, there needs to be a clear understanding on what eating disorders are; but for the general public this is no easy task, especially since health care professionals often struggle with the concept themselves.

Eating disorders – outcome measures

Whilst some outcome measures consensus has occurred within certain networks and regions, there is a lack of agreed outcome measures and associated data collection nationally. This is largely due to there being many opinions about how to measure eating disorder outcome and recovery. Unfortunately, we still lack a unified definition of 'recovery' and an agreement on how to measure it. Traditionally, changes in eating disorder symptomology and behaviours (both physiological and cognitive) are routinely monitored within services, with less emphasis being placed on level of functioning (e.g. family and social relationships, contribution to community, etc.) or qualitative aspects of life such as perception of recovery, which will be covered in more detail in Chapter 7.

The use of weight as an outcome measure

More often than not, weight restoration in the context of body mass index (BMI) or percentage median BMI is used within services. Certainly, as a dietitian, I [Sharleen] will never discredit the value in adequately re-nourishing the human body in order for it to perform optimally both on a physical and psychological level. However, it is important that weight is not used in isolation as a parameter of progress or recovery within eating disorders. This would be poor practice and might lead to multiple referrals and prove frustrating for the young person and their family.

Use of outcome questionnaires in eating disorders

Many questionnaires are available under the larger umbrella of adolescent mental health to aid formulation in eating disorders – for example, to monitor other dimensions such as anxiety, obsessive compulsive disorder (OCD), depression and family functioning. However, there are very few tools that are specifically for eating disorders, and those that exist have limitations to their use. One such questionnaire that is commonly used is described below.

EATING DISORDER EXAMINATION QUESTIONNAIRE (EDE-Q)

The EDE-Q, which is derived from the 'gold standard' Eating Disorder Examination Interview, is perhaps the single most widely used self-report measure of eating disorder symptoms. It provides a score on the global scale and comprises four subscales of postulated underlying psychopathology (restraint, eating concern, shape concern and weight concern) (Fairburn and Beglin 2008). Despite its widespread use in assessment and research, there is also a lot of literature outlining its limitations, some of which may be applicable to those with autism:

- The EDE-Q is much more pertinent to stereotypically feminine manifestations of body image disturbance. The sensitivity of the EDE-Q within the male population requires further evaluation as the questionnaire itself largely focuses on shape and weight concerns which are designed to assess a thinner body. Male body concerns, on the other hand, are often based on reversed paradigms, with an aspiration to increase muscularity and body mass (Lavender *et al.* 2010; Smith *et al.* 2017).

- This questionnaire may not be identifying eating disorders as much as it is identifying symptoms associated with eating disorders in people who may or may not have clinical eating disorders.

- Scores vary based on age and BMI; research shows that scores decrease with increasing age but increase with increasing weight even if an eating disorder is not present (Ro, Reas and Rosenvinge 2012).

- The EDE-Q does not fit well with the new *DSM-5* (American Psychiatric Association 2013) diagnoses.

- The questionnaire is based on a cognitive behaviour-focused model of eating disorders.

With these points in mind, it is important that the EDE-Q is not used in isolation when assessing for an eating disorder; indeed, a more in-depth exploration of the responses given is required in assessment to establish the context and aetiology of the problem.

AUTISM
What is autism?

Autism has been defined in various ways throughout the years. These definitions have come from experts with experience, clinicians and researchers. Claire Sainsbury, a woman with autism who is an accomplished author, writes: 'We are not people who just happen to have autism, it's not an appendage that can be separated from who we are as people, nor is it something shameful that has to be reduced to a sub clause' (Sainsbury 2000).

Current diagnostic criteria

The *DSM-5* (American Psychiatric Association 2013) and the *ICD-11* (World Health Organization 2018) specify one category for autism – autism spectrum disorder – in recognition of the variability of clinical presentation.

Timeline of definitions

Here is a timeline of definitions/labels/descriptions by some of the world's leading contributors, including individuals with autism, researchers and clinicians.

Dr Eugen Bleuler first used the term 'autistic' in 1908. Autism comes from the Greek word '*autos*', meaning self.

Leo Kanner, a psychiatrist from Austria-Hungary, described the young men he was studying as having 'a need for sameness…or a resistance to (unexpected) change' (Kanner 1943).

Hans Asperger (1944) described children with similar clinical features to Kanner's young people; however, Asperger's descriptions were different in the areas of communication, motor and fine skills, and in learning styles.

Wing and Gould (1979) provided the next major influential additions to research/literature and clinical practice when they published the 'triad of impairments', which grouped the features of autism, social interaction, communication and imagination and led to the understanding of difficulties with theory of mind. This led to the publication of *The Autistic Spectrum* (Wing 1996).

Temple Grandin's autobiography, *Emergence: Labeled Autistic* (Grandin and Scariano 1986), was the first autistic autobiography. This was followed in 2002 by *Nobody Nowhere* by **Donna Williams**. These two inspirational individuals pioneered the necessity for *collaboration with* and *listening to* autistic people in order to foster change in the way services are provided and how they are accessed, and how individuals receive appropriate, evidence-based specialist support.

Labels

The label argument continues to divide the autistic community, and the move to have positive descriptions of individuals is ever-changing.

We must remember that even though we have these descriptions/definitions, we are continually learning that there are different expressions of the commonalities. We see this with some girls and young women, and with a new generation of young men. We are now becoming better at identifying such individuals who don't specifically fit into the original Kanner/Asperger research definitions (which all related to boys) and who also *mask* (social camouflaging in order to manage their social anxiety).

Epidemiology of autism

The first studies of the prevalence of autism were undertaken in the 1960s and 1970s in Europe and the United States of America. At that time the prevalence was estimated in the range of 2–4 cases per 10,000 children; this was from results of an epidemiological study of children with the same behavioural pattern described by Lotter (1966), Rutter (2005) and Treffert (1970). The earliest prevalence studies found that boys were 3–4 times more likely to have autism than girls. When the diagnostic criteria for autism were widened in the 1980s and 1990s, autism prevalence studies around the world showed increases (Fombonne 2009; Miller *et al.* 2013; Rutter 2005).

This rise in prevalence can probably be attributed to the fact that at the end of the 20th century not only was there a widening of the diagnostic criteria but there was also the idea that autism is a spectrum of differences (Fombonne 2009; Miller *et al.* 2013; Wing and Potter 2002).

Other factors for consideration

In addition, there were other factors for consideration, such as clinicians having more access to training and resources and therefore being able to practise quality standardized research-based screening and assessments (Durkin *et al.* 2008; Miller *et al.* 2013; Schieve *et al.* 2011). Autism was also becoming something more present in the media. Routine screening was introduced into the medical profession and there was a better clinical understanding of comorbidities, termed 'diagnostic accrual'. There was also the introduction of the necessity for a diagnosis in order to receive appropriate services (Miller *et al.* 2013). The gathering of statistics in the 1990s also increased recognition, understanding and awareness of autism. Whilst we are still puzzled by many aspects of autism, there have been major advances in highlighting the genetic (Abrahams and Geschwind 2008), biological (Belmonte *et al.* 2004), potential controversial environmental (Currenti 2010), and developmental (Elsabbagh and Johnson 2010) origins of the condition.

As clinicians, we are improving in our identification of individuals with autism through informed screening and assessment. This is not only with girls and young women but also with boys and young men who present atypically. There is an older generation who are also being diagnosed in their later years. All this new data will inform the percentage and statistics of prevalence. The current ratio is approximately four males for every female (Werling and Gecshwind 2013).

In 1979 Lorna Wing and Judith Gould looked at the prevalence of autism, as defined by Leo Kanner. They found nearly 5 cases per 10,000, which was similar to the rate found by Lotter in 1966. Wing and Gould also looked at a different cohort of children (about 15 per 10,000) who had impairments of social interaction, communication and imagination (which Wing and Gould referred to as the triad of impairments), together with a repetitive stereotyped pattern of activities. They identified these children as being within the broader 'autism spectrum', bringing the total prevalence rate for autistic spectrum to approximately 20 in every 10,000 children.

In 1993, Ehlers and Gillberg published the results of a study which focused on the prevalence of Asperger syndrome and other autism profiles in children with an IQ of 70 or above. From the numbers of children they identified, they calculated a rate of 36 per 10,000 for those who definitely had Asperger syndrome, and another 35 per 10,000 for those who had social impairments but no diagnosis at that time.

There have been a number of epidemiological studies in different countries examining the prevalence of autism (but not the whole spectrum). These results range from 3.3 to 60.0 per 10,000, possibly due to differences/inconsistencies in definitions or case-finding methods (Wing and Potter 2002).

You can see that the earlier studies on prevalence focused on behavioural characteristics, which often included additional associations of severe language and cognitive delay. However, in the 1980s, different presentations of autism were recognized. These highlighted difficulties in the same clinical areas but without intellectual disability, and Asperger syndrome was introduced in the 1990s. Sub-categories were also introduced, such as atypical autism and pervasive developmental disorders unspecified (PDDU). Currently, the diagnostic term is autistic spectrum disorder. What was not previously included in the studies were the additional sensory difficulties which *DSM-5* (American Psychiatric Association 2013) now requires; therefore the impact of *DSM-5* changes remains to be fully assessed in the context of epidemiological surveys, and the span of case definition/identification and evaluation of autism is challenging researchers to obtain measurable rates.

The current prevalence is estimated above 1 in 100 (Brugha *et al.* 2012a), with studies of autism indicating that 1.1% of the population in the United Kingdom may be on the autism spectrum.

Autism – current pathways

Currently there is no standardized pathway in the United Kingdom. Pathways are sometimes led by health or education services or by local councils. Referrals and eligibility criteria for the pathways differ. The clinicians who assess the individuals and who sit on the diagnostic panels differ. The experience and skill set of the clinicians differ. How assessments are done can look very different (and that can even be within teams of the same clinical and service footprint). Some pathways sit across trusts in the same area and across clinical expertise, resulting in difficulties with communication and sharing of information about the individual and sometimes reassessments up to 2–3 times. The tools that are used vary as does the skill in the delivery of those assessments and measurement tools. Interpretation of information gathered differs, depending on training accessibility and also the availability of appropriately specialized staff. How the Autism Diagnostic Observation Schedule (ADOS) is delivered can vary, as can how the diagnosis is communicated to the individuals and their families. Waiting times can be anywhere from weeks to months to years, and some areas don't have access to support prior, during or after diagnosis.

NICE guidance

In December 2017, NICE reviewed their guideline, which now covers 'recognizing and diagnosing autism spectrum disorder in children and young people from birth up to 19 years. It also covers referral. It aims to improve the experience of children, young people and those who care for them'.

The recommendations included:

- local pathway for recognition
- referral and diagnostic assessment of possible autism
- recognizing children and young people with possible autism
- referring children and young people to the autism team
- autism diagnostic assessment for children and young people
- medical investigations
- communicating the results from the autism diagnostic assessment
- information and support for families and carers.

So, as you can see, *these are guidelines, not mandatory elements*, to be implemented in an autism diagnosis assessment and support and management. This is why each area interprets and implements what they can fund and what they decide is their local offer. Unfortunately, the current pathways that do exist often also miss many of the girls and young women. It's important to consider that if these individuals were identified and diagnosed earlier, we might not see them as frequently in the eating disorder services. What we are also learning now is that there is a cohort of boys and young men who mask in a similar way to girls, and who are also going under the radar for diagnosis. So although we are concerned that we are missing girls in terms of autism diagnosis, it is becoming more apparent that we are missing boys, too; it follows then that not only are we missing some boys through the autism assessment process, we are also missing boys in terms of eating disorders. These boys and young men are rarely seen in the eating disorder services so they could potentially and frighteningly be being missed twice.

From my [Fiona's] experience it is rare to seek advice and help from an eating disorder team if you are from a clinical background of autism. This is because if you are presented with a young person who is experiencing eating difficulties with a diagnosis of autism:

- It is rare to have access or be able to refer to such a specialist service, as although autism is recognized by eating disorder services, they would often refer the patient back, saying that the eating difficulties are in the context of the autism and are behavioural.

- The way the difficulties would be assessed would be through behavioural, cognitive communication and sensory assessments in the first instance, not through systemic and medical routes, which is the initial assessment route taken within eating disorder teams.

Currently, therefore, it is rare to find any pathways between the two specialisms; and even when there are pathways, they tend to consist of a passing to and from teams with little understanding of the link between the two or the function of the pathway. Neither team (eating disorders and autism) has cross-pollination of the respective specialist clinicians in order to support such referrals.

The specialists sit in separate teams and sometimes not even in the same buildings or trusts. Milton (2014) talks of the collaboration between researchers, clinicians and individuals with autism in the pathway planning to ensure that significant and momentous research scaffolds practical and meaningful systems of care.

Autism – outcome measures

In their paper, 'Autism spectrum disorders: A review of measures for clinical, health services and cost–effectiveness applications', Payakachat *et al.* talk about the need and increased interest in outcome measures for this population due to increasing prevalence:

> The prevalence of ASD increased over the last two decades from four to ten per 10,000 children between the 1980s and early 1990s, and then to 30 to 50 per 10,000 children in the early 2000s... School systems and medical care systems require increasing resources to treat the growing population of children diagnosed with ASD. Therefore, there is a considerable need for research on treatment strategies that ensure that children with ASDs achieve optimal outcomes. (Payakachat *et al.* 2012)

Considerations needed when asking for self-reporting or parental and other significant adult reporting particularly in this population are:

- How can we capture important data, particularly if the reporters we are relying on have difficulties with theory of mind?

- There need to be different ways of asking questions. How the reporters are asked to answer the questions also needs to be flexible. Clinicians need to be skilled in interpreting individualized ways of communicating with the individuals reporting.

- Is there a slant to the questions? For example, many are deficit-based and negative. We can understand people's difficulties by looking at their different ways of interacting and learning. Don't just consider what individuals can't do; look at what they can do. How is it different and why is this difference impacting on the global development/reaching of full potential of physical and emotional well-being?

- When asking significant adults to report on their child's/ teenager's differences, ask them in a way that represents how *their* child/teenager would respond.

- Be mindful that the significant adult in a young person's life may also have autism and difficulties with theory of mind. If so, then adjustments and understanding of this need to be factored in, and alternative ways of responding to the questions offered.

Clinical and behavioural outcome measures

There are numerous assessment tools which require descriptions and which assess the core symptoms and behavioural outcomes for children with ASD. Currently, as previously mentioned, the emphasis is on the negatives or the deficits. Although many of the instruments are used in clinical settings to describe the symptoms and impairments of autism for diagnostic purposes, they have been and continue to be used as outcome measures in research settings. The actual assessment tools will be discussed in Chapter 3.

Epidemiology of autism and eating disorders

Due to the complexities of ascertaining the prevalence of eating disorders in the United Kingdom, combined with an over-representation of autism symptoms in AN, there are difficulties determining the true occurrence of autism and eating disorders within the general population (Westwood and Tchanturia 2017). There is literature indicating that approximately 1 in 5 women with anorexia in eating disorder services also have autism (Mandy and Tchanturia 2015), and those presenting with both autism and anorexia have poorer outcomes than those who present with an eating disorder without autism (Arcelus *et al.* 2011).

Simon Baron-Cohen, in his paper 'Do girls with anorexia nervosa have elevated autistic traits?' concluded:

> While clinicians must continue to focus on low weight in patients with anorexia because this can be life-threatening, an understanding that some patients may have a different cognitive style, one prone to an obsessive focus on systems and a self-focused turning away from other people, may open up new avenues for both treatment and etiological research for anorexia. (Baron-Cohen *et al.* 2013)

Clinical psychologist Dr William Mandy (Elliott and Mandy 2018) has this to say:

> So, we know that if you look at people who are diagnosed with anorexia nervosa – people who are in various countries across Europe, who have been diagnosed with anorexia nervosa [and] who are receiving treatment – we find very, very high rates of undiagnosed autism amongst those people. Generally, 20 to 30 percent of people, of women, in studies of anorexia nervosa, if you actually assess them and think carefully about their social communication and their flexibility, you find that 20 to 30 percent of those women meet the criteria for autism.

As most of the research has leaned on autism and AN, there is minimal information or data on the frequency of autism in eating disorders such as BN, BED, OSFED and ARFID (Mansour *et al.* 2016; Nicely *et al.* 2014). Although there is an increased interest in autism in AN amongst clinicians and researchers, and indeed the journeys of those we share in this book are also of a restrictive nature (AN and ARFID), we must be considerate and not overlook that autism exists alongside other eating disorders where the presentation may differ considerably, making identification even more difficult.

CHAPTER 2

Journeys and Reflections

The following chapter introduces you to some amazingly resilient individuals who have agreed to share their experiences of their autism and eating disorders.

The first section features two young people: Niamh and Heidi. Niamh's story and the reflections of her mum, Mandy, are interwoven through our account of her care; and whilst Heidi is an anonymized case study, her journey gives us insight into how many young people with autism often present at eating disorder services. Identification of her autism led eating disorder practitioners to adapt treatment and interventions, through information and support provided by Fiona, which subsequently facilitated a nourished state and a better understanding of self.

We have chosen to provide a detailed overview of these journeys of care early on in the book, so that you can actively reflect as we walk you through their treatment and interventions. It is the lived experiences of our young people with autism and eating disorders through services that will reshape the way that we work with them and provide the foundations for better-quality care and pathways.

The second section introduces Ruth, Kay and Jake who have very kindly agreed to share their experiences of services from an adult's perspective. This enables us to try to understand the impact on them of understanding and managing their difficulties. It is imperative that we, as clinicians, listen to individuals who are experts by experience, in order to promote and evoke service change. Listening to adults' reflections on their experiences informs our practice, enabling us to understand, support and enable our young people who are currently needing understanding and support.

The majority of people who present with eating disorders and autism to our service do so because of the associated physical health risks, and it just so happens that the journeys and reflections from the young people and adults who share their stories in this book have restrictive eating disorders. We acknowledge that other eating disorders may present differently in those with autism.

YOUNG PEOPLE'S JOURNEYS

NIAMH

Niamh is currently 16 years old and has been known to CAMHS since the age of 12. She originally presented with eating difficulties and was under the eating disorder service for 1 year and 9 months. Six months after discharge from the eating disorder team, Niamh was re-referred to CAMHS, and it was during this episode of care that autism was diagnosed.

Niamh told us that she does not remember a lot of what happened, so has recalled as much as she can, with her mum (with consent from Niamh) helping out with the other details. Although there is no definite answer as to why, having no recollection or memory of a period of starvation is something that is commonly reported by those who have experienced restrictive eating disorders. Likewise, specific memory difficulties are common within the field of autism, due to a lack of communication between the reasoning and memory systems of the brain.

Niamh says:

> People always said I was a 'quirky' child. I hated that word. It wasn't an insult; people said it with smiles on their faces, but it felt like a punch to the gut. Why wasn't I normal? I tried hard to fit in, but no matter how hard I tried it didn't work. Other children called me weird. I didn't know what made me weird. I didn't understand. High school was awful for me. I didn't know anybody there. I didn't know the school. It was scary and cold and loud. I was completely overwhelmed. I didn't know what to do. I wanted to disappear. Food gave me something to think about and to obsess over. I knew

how many calories were in everything I ate and exactly how much I weighed. Whittling down those numbers made me feel sheltered and safe. After a while I realized that what was happening was serious. People gave me worried looks, my face started to look gaunt, girls at school commented on how skinny I was. I started to get scared and ended up talking to my mum. She told me about CAMHS, and after some phone calls she told me they currently had no room for me and I would be put on a waiting list.

Mandy reflects on her daughter:

Niamh first became involved with services in 2014. I had noticed some weight loss over the summer but thought perhaps she had grown taller. She'd always been slight, so it wasn't a big concern. She was a dancer and all the girls were thin. Then I took photographs at our annual Halloween party of all the children stood together. Looking at them afterwards, I saw how thin and sad she looked. I had a sudden feeling that something was very wrong. I took her to see our GP and she had lost 11 pounds since she had last been weighed and measured at primary school. I was horrified. We were referred to CAMHS and sent home. From then on the decline was rapid. I was in a constant state of panic as I tried and failed to feed her. She would say, 'I've already eaten', 'I have tummy ache', 'I'm not hungry'. The excuses were endless. We were suddenly arguing about how many chickpeas were in her lunch box. I got a phone call to say she had fainted at school. I sat her down and told her how worried I was and she cried and said she would try harder, but it just seemed to fuel the fire and she got worse. The list of acceptable foods became ridiculous. Her physical condition continued to deteriorate to the point that her sister would cry when she saw her. We would spend ages in the supermarket and everything was 'not an option'. It was like she was in self-destruct mode and nothing would stop her. We were seen at Leigh Infirmary and referred to the eating disorder team.

I rang CAMHS and was told the assessment was in December but I lost the plot and said I didn't think we had long. It sounds very dramatic now, but it was the truth. Thankfully we were listened to and we saw the consultant paediatrician, in mid-November.

From that point on, Niamh was obsessed with the number on the scale. I was amazed at her knowledge of food, calories and grams of fat, and became confused as to what was the eating disorder and what was just Niamh. Looking back, I think the build-up to this was very gradual. I wasn't sure how long she had actually been like this. She started to eat everything with a spoon and nibble at the edges of crumpets. I couldn't say when this all started but food and eating took over our lives. Niamh would cook and bake, read cookery books and watch Jamie Oliver on repeat. Her idols became Ella (from *Deliciously Ella*) or recovered girls [i.e. girls who had recovered from eating disorders] on Instagram. She researched things online constantly. She had been vegetarian for years but then she wanted to be vegan and then raw vegan.

Assessment

Due to the organizational structure at the time of referral, Niamh underwent two assessments: a 'front door' assessment by the Primary Child Mental Health team, who then referred her for a specialist eating disorder assessment.

As you explore the following information that was collated at Niamh's assessments, we invite you to reflect and consider what could have been done differently. Was information provided that required more analysis, exploration or context? Was there anything missing from the information collected? We have deliberately included such detail at this stage of the book in order to provoke your curiosity and initiate your personal reflection about the processes that these young people underwent. We will explore these points further with you in Chapter 3, which covers assessments, and in Chapter 4 where we discuss identification and formulation.

First assessment

The purpose of this 'front door' assessment was to establish the 'best fit' level of care for Niamh's needs at that time. Niamh was assessed by a single practitioner, who established that Niamh had made 'adjustments' to her dietary intake in the previous 10 months, initially converting to vegetarianism, which later became established as restricting further food types and quantities. There were indications that the reason for Niamh becoming vegetarian had changed over time, but this was not further explored. It also highlighted that Niamh had 'entrenched' thoughts, adhering to a set of rigid and restrictive rules around food and not wanting to become fat. She was experiencing physical health symptoms such as tiredness, fainting and feeling full (resulting in refusal to eat). There were no purging or bingeing behaviours. There was very little exploration of who Niamh was prior to the 'problem', apart from her mum describing Niamh as a 'sensitive' young person who 'personalizes her friendship problems', isolating herself from her peers, and a person who is 'self-critical, a worrier and a perfectionist'.

Based on the information gathered at this assessment, Niamh was appropriately referred to the specialist eating disorder team for a further assessment.

Eating disorder assessment

Historically and currently, eating disorder assessments vary in approach and content across the country, an aspect we discuss in more detail in Chapter 3. However, their primary focus is to explore the eating difficulty in more depth and to ascertain whether it meets the criteria of an eating disorder. Niamh was further assessed approximately 1 month after her first assessment.

The following information was collated:

- *History and behaviours associated with eating difficulties:* There was a change in eating habits prior to Niamh commencing secondary school. She made a conscious effort to be healthy, becoming vegetarian and eating foods that her mother would eat (mum was on a 'diet'). When Niamh started high school, her food variety and portion sizes further reduced with a concurrent reduction in appetite. At the time of assessment Niamh was described as a 'control freak', always reading the back of food packets, although further detail on what Niamh was specifically looking at was not shared. She worried a lot about meals and food in terms of timings of meals, what food was being provided and how it was being cooked.

These worries meant that Niamh was not socializing, as she would not engage in any activity that included food or eating out. There was a note that Niamh engaged in excessive exercise in the spare room, but this was not further elaborated on.

- *Body image:* There appeared to be a lot of confusion in terms of Niamh's body image. She was able to recognize that she was thin and not fat. She alluded to the fact that it was more about the weight and not how she looked; she had been highly aware of her weight prior to secondary school and this awareness had then intensified, based on her changing oral intake. Niamh reports 'freaking out' when she gained 1 pound after eating burger, chips and foods from vending machines, and being really happy when she went down to 80 pounds after a day of having two sips of banana smoothie and two lettuce leaves. Niamh also shared that she was surprised at how her body looked without clothes and that she was able to see that she had a 'big' stomach and thighs. Niamh was reported to have strong self-esteem – liking who she was.

- *Developmental history:* Niamh was born at full term (there was a query about Down syndrome). As a baby, she was described as a poor sleeper (she would only sleep when lying on a parent) and also a poor feeder (she did not like milk). She was slow to talk and to point to things, and was referred to as an 'odd toddler' as she used to scream and screech, which her parents became accustomed to. At the age of 2, there was less of an observed delay in developmental milestones. Niamh struggled to make friends when starting primary school and this persisted until Year 3 when she made two friends. Friendships changed when Niamh commenced secondary school, where she made a lot of close friends; however, these friendships remained strained. Niamh had expressed wishes to be home-schooled. In terms of personality, Niamh was described as very independent, strong-minded, obsessive and someone who didn't like change.

Diagnosis

Based on the information shared at this assessment, Niamh was diagnosed with anorexia nervosa – restrictive type (because she restricted food, leading to significant weight loss). Although there was evidence that Niamh had strong preoccupations with food and believed that if she ate certain foods she would get fat, she did not show evidence of a distorted body image.

Treatment/Intervention

> Eventually I ended up with a team, a therapist I quite liked and a doctor who told me my heart would stop if I carried on. That scared me.
>
> — *(Niamh)*

Niamh engaged in a multi-modal package of care with the eating disorder team, which included psychiatry review, individual appointments with a senior nurse practitioner, dietetic reviews, and frequent therapeutic appointments with a clinical psychologist.

Psychological input

Intervention with the clinical psychologist who assessed Niamh was what Niamh found most helpful during her time with the eating disorder team. Goal-orientated sessions with the clinical psychologist provided Niamh with a space to talk through her problems and collaboratively establish solutions. The clinical psychologist used an externalizing approach to address the eating disorder (further discussed in Chapter 6), where Niamh named her illness 'Mario'. This was to enable Niamh to challenge previously held beliefs around food.

> They told me to give my anorexia a name; they talked about it like it was a demon living inside me. I thought it was stupid.
>
> — *(Niamh)*

Dietetic input

I [Sharleen] first met Niamh when I joined the service 6 months after she was diagnosed with an eating disorder. Our sessions were often short (30 minutes instead of the usual 60 minutes, according to Niamh's preference) and were largely led by Niamh and what she wanted to discuss. At the first session, Niamh and her mother had agreed between them that Niamh would follow a vegan diet (there is more about this in Chapter 6).

Discharge

Niamh remained stable in terms of her physical restoration and was subsequently discharged from the eating disorder team when the psychologist also left the trust.

> When the psychologist was moved from the team, I knew that was it for us. Niamh didn't have the energy to start to build yet another relationship again, and the general consensus was that she no longer met the criteria for the eating disorder team. We were discharged. I knew it wasn't the right thing – everyone was commenting on how well she looked, but deep down I knew we'd be back.
>
> — *(Mandy)*

Re-referral

Six months after Niamh was discharged from the eating disorder service, she was re-referred by her GP because she was:

- experiencing feelings of low mood (emotionally flat with no enjoyment in her life)

- struggling to sleep

- feeling anxious

- isolating herself

- lacking in motivation (stopped doing the things she used to enjoy)

- secretive about eating.

Assessment

> Everything seemed ok for a while. I was healthy. I could manage on my own. Slowly, I started to realize how empty I felt. I was eating but I cried every day. I didn't enjoy anything. I didn't want to get out of bed. Every day felt like a struggle and I couldn't understand why. We realized I shouldn't have left CAMHS, I was far from ok, but they had no room for me. I would have to wait.
>
> ———— *(Niamh)*

Niamh underwent a second 'front door' assessment 1 month after the second referral to CAMHS. There were no reported concerns regarding Niamh's eating at this time; however, it was acknowledged that Niamh had ongoing difficulties with mood that had not resolved. Niamh, at this time, continued to be home-schooled (because of reported anxiety about attending school), but she was also attending a college once a week to support her transition to a sixth form college. Niamh found this attendance stressful – she felt different at college and that no one liked her.

Niamh appeared distracted and hypervigilant in this assessment, avoiding eye contact with the practitioner. She shared that she always felt different, felt she had no control of her emotions and at times felt out of control, which often manifested as extreme mood swings. Niamh expressed how she had no enjoyment in life. She said she did not feel normal (although she was unsure of what normal feels like as she just felt empty). Niamh's mother confirmed that as early as 7 years old Niamh had asked what was wrong with her. Niamh's mother also confirmed that Niamh appeared to look depressed and sad from a young age, even though there was no reason for this. Niamh also shared that she had ritualistic behaviours before going to sleep in order to help with her anxiety and that her sleep patterns were abnormal.

Niamh was accepted by CAMHS and transferred from the Single Point of Access assessment team into Generic CAMHS (integrated mental health services for young people) for further support.

CAMHS

It was at the first session with Niamh's care co-ordinator Emilie (see Emilie's observations and thoughts in Chapter 4) that autism was suspected and a consultation was sought with Fiona regarding this.

> Things could have been very different for Niamh had it not been for Emilie. I really felt that I was really listened to for the first time and Niamh clicked with her straight away. I would say that Emilie was the first person we had spoken to with a genuine interest in what was going on. She wanted to know the nitty gritty, to get to the root of the problems Niamh was having. She had a gut feeling and ran with it. It scares me to think where Niamh would be had that not happened. Niamh was honest and open with her, which surprised me, but somehow her questions seemed relevant and made Niamh want to talk about herself.
>
> —————— (Mandy)

I [Fiona] vividly remember meeting Niamh for the first time. At 14 years old she was self-assured, direct and controlled the appointment. By that I mean she was clear with me as to what she would discuss and what she wouldn't; she told me when she thought my questions were irrelevant or patronizing or going over old ground. She became visibly tired very quickly and lost concentration and motivation to remain in the conversation and in the room.

She was so obviously intelligent. I remember feeling delighted to be in the presence of a great mind whilst also feeling a little like she was waiting for me to mess up. Her vulnerability and fear were palpable, and what was more obvious was that she had little understanding that I could feel that from her.

At that point I knew that if we could find out how to understand Niamh, then with the support of her family and her wonderfully insightful and brave mum, she would go on to be the best she could be physically, mentally, emotionally and academically.

She had already forged a positive therapeutic relationship with Emilie, a senior nurse practitioner, so introducing me as yet another person asking questions in the long line of clinicians whom she had already encountered in her CAMHS journey was challenging and daunting for both Niamh and me.

I began the task of discussing and exploring autism with Niamh and her mum, whilst also trying to support and understand Niamh in relation to her significant generalized and social anxiety and low mood. Emilie and I did a gradual transition of care as it was important that Niamh had a person involved with her whom she trusted and liked whilst establishing a new and different therapeutic relationship with myself.

> When we met Fiona I felt straight away that she 'got' Niamh and that Niamh would get the help she needed. We both felt listened to and understood. Niamh's eventual diagnosis of ASC has been the most positive thing that has happened for us as a family. Fiona has supported Niamh to feel more confident and to be herself, to not want to hide away. I don't actually know what they talk about in their sessions but I do know that they have benefited Niamh massively.
>
> *(Mandy)*

The information above from both the clinician and Niamh, and its relevance to the need to shift clinical practice, will be discussed in more detail in Chapters 3 and 4.

HEIDI

Heidi is currently 16 years old and presented to the eating disorder service 2 years ago in physical health crisis. She accessed the hospital Accident and Emergency (A&E) unit due to concerns regarding rapid and significant weight loss (although she remained in the 'healthy' range), blackouts, fainting, low blood pressure, low pulse rate and chest pain. It is not unusual for those with an eating disorder such as AN to present in crisis, and from my [Sharleen's] personal experience, those with autism and/or ARFID are even more likely to do so. Heidi was admitted to a paediatric ward for physical stabilization, where the paediatrician referred Heidi urgently to the community eating disorder team who assessed Heidi on the ward. She did not have a diagnosis of autism at the time of this assessment; it only became apparent as practitioners explored the context of her problems.

Eating disorder assessment

Heidi was assessed by a multi-disciplinary team (MDT) consisting of a family therapist, a child and adolescent consultant psychiatrist, a nurse practitioner and myself [Sharleen], a dietitian. The pros and cons of this type of multi-disciplinary assessment will be discussed in Chapter 3. Heidi struggled to engage in parts of the assessment and although she was offered time alone with one of the practitioners, she declined as she reported that talking about food was stressful for her. The following information was gathered at this time:

History and behaviours associated with eating difficulties

From Heidi's mum's perspective, Heidi began restricting her diet 'out of the blue' with no previous concerns regarding her eating apart from 'normal' fussy eating when she was a toddler. Heidi shared that she developed concerns regarding eating after a healthy eating talk by her teacher in school. Thereafter, the amount and types of food she would eat reduced, and Heidi would not allow her mum to prepare and cook meals. Heidi's change in eating patterns led to weight loss. She found herself being pleased about this as she suddenly but briefly felt better about herself (she reported that people had previously made comments about her weight and stature calling her 'big', 'sturdy' and 'well-built'). In an effort to continue to feel good about herself, Heidi started to research about weight loss online and this subsequently led her to calorie counting. Heidi found calorie counting soothing and relaxing and was pleased when she was managing to eat the 'allowed' or 'permitted' (based on Heidi's own thoughts) number of calories for that day.

Heidi's mum reported that Heidi was taking a long time to eat – for example, over 3 hours to eat a small snack such as a cereal bar, which meant that subsequent meals would be missed. Heidi reported that she didn't feel hungry and that when she did eat she struggled with feelings of fullness (early satiety) which felt uncomfortable and impacted on daily functioning for her.

Heidi did not engage in excessive exercise nor did she take any medication/laxatives to aid with weight loss. However, there were concerns from her mum that Heidi was purging (making herself sick) after meals. Heidi denied that she was doing this and became highly distressed (shouting and crying) at the implication. Nursing staff reported that Heidi was taking a long time in the bathroom after meals, despite efforts to manage this behaviour whilst on the ward.

Body image

Heidi was unhappy with how she looked, although she denied having a target weight and did not weigh herself. She was able to identify that she had lost a lot of weight but was fearful of 'getting fat'. She was able to state that her focus was more on aesthetics (how she thought she looked) than her weight (number on the scale) and wished to continue to lose weight until she was happy with herself.

Developmental history

Information on developmental history was not taken at the assessment. This may have been the result of Heidi presenting in crisis on the paediatric ward. (Emergencies can mean there is limited time and space to complete a full assessment.) Unfortunately, this can mean that aspects such as developmental history are not explored and therefore the formulation is not fully informed (this will be considered further in Chapter 4).

Other

Heidi was described by her mum as a 'worrier'. Heidi also expressed wishes to end her life and said that she engaged in self-harming. She described having 'confused feelings' which would result in mood swings and violent outbursts towards family and friends (this had been occurring for a number of months prior to the eating difficulties). Heidi was feeling left out and rejected by friends as a result of what she described as 'communication difficulties', and this had begun when she transitioned to high school. Heidi did not further elaborate on this within the assessment.

Diagnosis

Heidi was diagnosed with a depressive disorder and atypical anorexia nervosa after her eating disorder assessment.

Treatment/Intervention

Early intervention

The initial treatment plan for Heidi was refeeding and physical stabilization whilst she was on the paediatric ward. Unfortunately, due to her feelings of hopelessness, issues with satiety and distress around food, Heidi required nasogastric feeding (feeding via a tube that enters via the nose and into the stomach). She was also not engaging therapeutically with the team, therefore it was agreed that she would be referred to a specialist eating disorder inpatient unit (SEDU). After 4 weeks on the paediatric ward, Heidi was accepted to a SEDU and spent 9 months at this unit.

Medication

Heidi was started on 10 mg fluoxetine due to her depressive disorder and this was increased to 20 mg. (Through discussion about Heidi's sensory needs, it was established that she felt able to consider taking a medication if it was available in liquid form, such as fluoxetine. This topic is discussed further in Chapter 6.)

Inpatient care

Full details of Heidi's inpatient stay cannot be shared as this episode of care is not managed by the community team. Heidi's community care co-ordinator did attend regular Care Programme Approach (CPA) meetings, where updates of her care were provided. Heidi remained on nasogastric feeding for a couple of months whilst on the SEDU, often requiring hold practices in order for this to occur. It was shared that because of distress around mealtimes, Heidi increased her self-harming behaviours whilst on the SEDU. Using a goal-based approach Heidi transitioned to an oral liquid diet, using oral nutritional supplements as her main source of nutrition, which needed to be given in fixed amounts at set times. She was unable to move towards food while she was an inpatient, so after initial reservations the community team agreed to manage her care in an outpatient setting.

Outpatient care (community services)

Upon discharge, Heidi still struggled with her body image and eating food (she was discharged on a liquid diet), and she continued to have fleeting thoughts of self-harm and wanting to end her life. She initially engaged in family therapy with Sam, with whom she had established a good relationship whilst on the paediatric ward, and she was subsequently reintroduced to dietetic input and cognitive behavioural therapy (CBT), full details of which will be covered in Chapter 6. Throughout this process, Heidi was also seen individually by her care co-ordinator, who managed her overall care.

You may have noticed that Heidi's care package was a lot more comprehensive than Niamh's in terms of the number of professionals who were involved. This was a direct result of the access and wait times, where increased funding meant more resources for the service. This said, never underestimate the power of a therapeutic relationship as trust in even one practitioner may mean that the person will be willing to engage with the wider team.

PSYCHIATRY INPUT

Heidi's medication was regularly reviewed by the team psychiatrist and this was an area where formulation (discussed in Chapter 4) could be revisited.

DIETETIC INPUT

Heidi's initial contact with me [Sharleen] was on the paediatric ward when she required refeeding and then nasogastric feeding. As a result of this, the initial relationship between us was strained.

There are ethical considerations when using a nasogastric tube, which are further reviewed in Chapter 6. The combination of Heidi's depressive disorder, strong eating disorder cognitions and her compromised physical health led to the team and family's decision to proceed with nasogastric feeding. The immediacy with which this needed to happen meant that I didn't have the opportunity to get to know Heidi enough to understand her relationship with food and the role her eating disorder served.

Despite efforts to connect with Heidi during her paediatric admission, she did not wish to engage in any individual work with me until after her discharge from the SEDU. I continued to review her nutritional progress while she was on the paediatric ward via the nursing staff and my eating disorder colleagues.

After discharge from the inpatient unit, Heidi did not initially want to see me as she felt that she was not ready. I eventually joined the family sessions, and it was through these joint sessions that autism was suspected (more on this in Chapter 4). This led to Fiona being consulted on the best way to work with Heidi. Heidi transitioned to a full diet of food, in what was not an easy journey (see Chapter 6). Heidi then set about challenging herself in terms of her 'feared foods' and subsequently her 'dietary rules'. The CBT therapist and I worked collaboratively with Heidi on these, always letting Heidi set the pace.

Discharge

Nine months after discharge from the SEDU, Heidi made the transition to a full diet consisting of a wide variety of foods. She recognized, however, that she did require reassurance at times from her mum or dad in order to keep going with this. Heidi and her parents also had a better understanding of who Heidi was and how to approach various aspects of her life. In view of this, it was agreed that Heidi should be discharged from the service. She was still on the autism pathway at the point of discharge from the eating disorder team, and was diagnosed with autism at a later date.

ADULTS REFLECT ON THEIR JOURNEYS

RUTH
'Autism and anorexia – reflections on experiences of treatment'

The lead-up to my illness: I was always the outsider, the 'weirdo', not fitting in, the one that got talked about/laughed at behind their back,

I was outspoken when it came to people breaking rules, I worked too fast, I wasn't able to take part in social activities.

I had given up chocolate as part of a charity challenge and this led to me starting to restrict other types of food. If I could feel in control of something, it made everything else feel less overwhelming.

The eating disorder got worse at this stage and I eventually became very unwell. I had bought scales to weigh myself with and became obsessed with the number going down. I continued to eat but I tried to offset everything I ate with exercise. I was so obsessed with the numbers that I remember being surprised when my clothes became too big for me – it was like my brain hadn't computed that the number going down would alter my appearance. I bought a fitness tracker, which further fuelled my obsession with the numbers. I'd set myself arbitrary numbers of steps I'd need to walk each day, and how many exercises I would also need to do. My disorder was never about appearance; I have no vanity or care for how I look.

On reflection, I've always been a low weight. When I was a child, I struggled with rigidity around what I would eat, often not feeling hungry due to anxiety. I didn't like certain textures or smells of food. I was regularly bullied for being different and about my appearance. I remember thinking at the time, 'At least I am thin', but my behaviours around food were not from a desire to lose weight. My dad also struggled with the smells of certain foods and ate a rigid diet, so it wasn't until I became a teenager that I had opportunities to try certain foods such as curry, pasta, stir fries, etc. when at friends' houses.

KAY
'What shaped my relationship with food?'

My childhood was in the 1970s. I was characterized as a quiet child. In reality my heartfelt wish was to fade into the background in any situation to avoid the discomfort of not feeling able to function socially.

Physically, I was a small, submissive child with long blonde hair, known to my family as bright and intelligent but forever struggling to eat due to anxiety. Later in life I was diagnosed with a condition that affects the digestive system called hypermobile Ehlers-Danlos syndrome (EDS).

Emotionally, I found growing up as a female traumatic, and as an autistic child my emotions felt locked away. It may sound silly but I remember my father watching the film *Seven Brides for Seven Brothers*, a Technicolor musical that was supposed to be happy and uplifting. As my father warbled along to the songs, it became clear to me that abducting women and forcing them to become 'house slaves' is perfectly normal and socially acceptable. My female autistic mask was forming as I asked myself over and over, 'How am I going to survive into adulthood?' The answer came back as a snapshot of an unchanging, thin, submissive woman. I never remember anyone in my childhood ever asking me, 'How are you? Are you feeling safe, do you feel scared?'

The 1980s was a cruel time physically for any woman, regardless of autism. We were reduced to coat hangers underneath big shoulder pads and hair; we could never be thin enough.

My eating problems started when I was 14. I was a late developer and did not start my periods until the Christmas just before I was 15. From a sensory viewpoint, I detested the way the smell of my body changed, but no one else seemed to notice this. I felt exhausted, like I was going through an ordeal simply for having a female body. If I had known I had inherited Von Willebrand's disease from my father and simply bled much more than most other women every month, instead of being told by doctors, 'It is normal, just get on with it', I might have received some help. Communicating with medical professionals has proved very challenging over the years; my expressionless face and quietly spoken demeanour, which I maintain even when very distressed, has not served me well.

By the next Christmas, events colluded to create the perfect conditions to manifest the eating disorder I subsequently struggled with for many years to come. I was socially isolated, continuing to come to terms with the changes my body had made in its attempts to develop into an adult; in my opinion it was not doing a good job as my hips were too big and my breasts too small. I found myself fighting off a really bad stomach bug. My mum bought me kaolin and morphine over the counter, and I was ill for weeks. To my relief, it meant I missed a lot of stress by not being strong enough to go to school, and I stopped having periods. In the end I became bed-bound, weighing less than 6 stone. I felt very happy. I was away from the hell of school and my goal to somehow become thin had come to fruition. Now all I needed to do to survive was to maintain this.

JAKE

Jake is currently 19 years old and although he continues to have services in his life, he is studying and learning to drive. I [Fiona] knew Jake when he was at primary school and have watched him grow into a wonderful person. He has a strong, loving, supportive family and a network of people around him, whom he truly appreciates.

Jake and his mum have provided some insightful explanations that we need to take into consideration when working in the field of autism and eating disorders:

Jake tells us:

> I find it far less stressful if I can eat food when I'm ready, in my own time, and make my own choices. I find it stressful if I'm given a plate of food and expected to eat it. I'm not sure why that is.
>
> I've realized on my journey that having parents that have helped me and spoken up for me to get me the right support has made all the difference. I also found a great support worker in school that treated me as a normal person and encouraged me to do age-appropriate activities, including the importance of looking after myself with fitness and health. This gave me confidence to do other activities. I now see other people with the same difficulties that haven't had the support of their family, and their lives are very different to mine now.

Samantha, Jake's mum, tells us about her son:

> Jake was diagnosed with ASD in May 2009. The reason for late diagnosis? The SENCo [special educational needs co-ordinator] at school disagreed that Jake was displaying signs of ASD, and in her opinion it was behaviour. This was despite Jake being made to sit on a table alone in the hallway outside the headmaster's office

because of his outbursts in the dinner hall. During break, Jake could not interact with other pupils and would have to play in a marked-out area with another boy who had similar outbursts.

Food and eating... From a young age, Jake drank large amounts of milk, and it was very difficult for him to transition from his bottle to a beaker or cup. As he was overweight, I had to gradually dilute the milk with water as milk was the only thing he would drink and often replaced food with milk. When Jake began eating a wider variety of solid foods, he was always very sensory in the way he would squish the food between his hands and eat with his hands. He also had strange combinations of foods, e.g. dipping chips in yogurts.

By the time he reached the age of 3 to 4, he began wanting his foods all separated on the plate, with nothing touching. If anything did touch or overlap, he would become very distressed and refuse to eat it. We solved this problem by putting the foods in separate dishes. Jake would also refuse to use a spoon or fork, and ate with his hands, even if it was not finger foods but sloppy foods instead. We tried numerous types of cutlery, but he refused to use any of them.

Jake would not eat when out (e.g. in a café) if he had seen the person serving the food physically touch the food. He also preferred extremes of hot or freezing foods. Instead of eating sweets, he would crunch ice for hours each evening. He was also obsessed with a hatred of dust and so all his drinks would have to be in drinking sports bottles to prevent any specks of dust contaminating them.

Jake also had a lot of digestive problems, and still does – lots of foods give him indigestion or a burning sensation in his mouth and throat. He was also very sensitive to food additives, especially a yellow food colouring called 'annatto'. If he had this, he would be very energetic and have outbursts of behaviour that would leave him distressed, upset and sweating. This could last for up to 3 days following eating a yellow food.

Jake would also overeat as he would never feel full, despite eating large quantities of high-carb foods. We tried smaller portions and allowing 30 minutes before giving him any more but his brain would never send the signals to tell him he was full or hungry. Between the ages of 10 and 14, Jake gained a large amount of weight due to this. He was encouraged to go to the gym and was introduced to a personal trainer. To complement this, Jake was given a structured food plan that involved weighing portions and eating a healthy, balanced meal. As this gave Jake more control over his foods, he stuck to this and would only eat the foods on his food planner with no cheats. Jake lost 3 stone and to this day sticks to a very healthy set diet that complements his gym workouts.

Jake is now almost 19 and his eating habits have totally changed. He will only eat because he has to and not for enjoyment. His eating also depends greatly on his mood or how tired he is. He is tired most of the time and needs reminding to eat. I still prepare food for Jake and leave it in the fridge for him to warm up when he's ready to eat. He likes to be in control of his own eating and eats when he chooses rather than when he's told. He also plans his eating around his activities for the day. If it's a gym day, he's very focused on eating well; if it's just a quiet day, he will hardly eat. Jake no longer crunches on ice but he drinks large amounts of ice-cold water. He still has lots of indigestion problems, despite removing food groups. This could be down to high anxiety and the effects it has on the body.

From these individuals' descriptions of their autism and eating difficulties/disorders, we can see the very different clinical presentations for each of them but also the elements of clinical similarity. We can see that the ways in which they manage their challenges differ and are very individual. Acknowledging that what works for one person may not necessarily work for another is necessary in this area; however, there may be core similarities which prove that certain strategies can be individualized in order to be effective.

CHAPTER 3

Assessment

'The beginning is the most important part of the work.'

(Plato, c.427 BC–c.347 BC)

Assessments are the foundation to our understanding of our young people. They therefore need to be undertaken by clinicians skilled in the area of assessment, with access to the appropriate evidence-based screening tools to enable them to highlight markers or indicators which will then inform the next stage of assessment. That stage of assessment should be executed by clinicians in the identified specialist fields. There are often different layers and stages of assessment for our young people.

BEFORE THE ASSESSMENT

Assessments can often (but unfortunately not always) be lengthy sessions, ranging from 1 to 3 hours, depending on service processes and the complexity of the presentation. Often, young people and their families are understandably anxious about coming to mental health services and wonder what will happen when they are there. Indeed, we have had young people thinking that they were going to be 'taken away', but although we have had to send young people to A&E because of physical health concerns, as in Heidi's case, this is the exception, not the rule. Outlining the amount of time the assessment will take and giving some basic process information, including who will be present, in the initial appointment letter is a means of reducing apprehension and worry prior to the assessment. Ruth shares below how her assessment differed and how she struggled with appointments.

I had a quick assessment with the eating disorder service, because of my low weight. I struggled with appointments for the following reasons:

- lack of written information

- lack of consistency around sending me written details of our appointments

- noise during appointments

- the person I was seeing making agreements with me and not sticking to them.

— *(Ruth)*

As in Niamh's case, young people have often undergone multiple mental health assessments by different teams and find themselves telling their story over and over again. The publication of the access and waiting time standards for children and young people has meant that this process has somewhat changed, so that now, any referral indicating eating difficulties and weight loss is screened directly by the eating disorder team in order to prevent delays and reassessment. Unfortunately, this is not to say that multiple assessments do not occur in the current system, as eating difficulties may only be flagged at the initial generic mental health assessment. Having multiple assessments has been highlighted by families as frustrating and time-consuming, even more so for those with autism or suspected autism. Therefore, we still need to be mindful as practitioners of the impact this has on young people and their families – effective information gathering before the assessment and allowing flexibility within the assessment process will minimize such frustrations.

THE EATING DISORDER ASSESSMENT

The purpose of any mental health assessment is to build up a picture of a person's mental health needs; however, there is great variability in how this is achieved across the United Kingdom as there is limited literature on what type of assessment method is more effective.

Unfortunately, this inconsistency is also true in eating disorder assessments. Some services use generic mental health assessments, whilst others use specialist assessments that focus more intensely on food and compensatory behaviours and the relationship with food. Assessments are completed either by a single mental health practitioner or by a multi-disciplinary team (the latter means there is a range of differing professionals from both physical and mental health backgrounds) completing the assessment with the young person and their family. The pros and cons of each method (single practitioner versus MDT) are as follows:

Single practitioner assessment
Pros

- Reduces anxiety for the young person being assessed.

- Assessments are often shorter in length.

- Improves ability to develop relationship. (As you will recall from Chapter 2, Niamh was assessed by a single practitioner, who went on to provide individual therapy to Niamh and was considered an important factor in Niamh's eating disorder recovery.)

- Allows greater flexibility in terms of diary co-ordination.

Cons

- Reliant on the confidence, skills and experience of the practitioner (intra-individual variability).

- Diagnosis and formulation are often delayed until the presentation has been discussed with the wider team.

MDT assessment
Pros

- Different areas of expertise allow for a more holistic view of the young person, contributing to a wide-angle formulation.

- One of the practitioners can take an observer role.

- Diagnosis and formulation can often be shared at the end of the assessment.

- More accurate information can be shared, because of the profession being represented (e.g. dietetics, psychiatry).

Cons

- Can increase the anxiety of the young person being assessed.

- Can often increase the time of the assessment.

- Is resource-intensive and requires co-ordination.

- Establishing a relationship can be more difficult.

In the team that I [Sharleen] work with, assessments are multi-disciplinary and therefore I admittedly have a bias towards this structure. That said, MDT flexibility is key to a successful assessment and establishing a therapeutic relationship. When an MDT works well together, establishing the needs of the young person prior to the assessment (ironically, gathering information before the formal information-gathering process), it can create a safe and calm environment.

Eating disorders are complex, especially when combined with autism or suspected autism. The dynamics of the MDT can still be present but not visible via the means of a two-way mirror; or the structure of the assessment can alter where there is a combination of both MDT and single-practitioner time with the young person and/or family. Such considerations will be covered in more detail in Chapter 8.

Ultimately, assessments gather information based on a snapshot in time. This ensures that the current problem is acknowledged and the appropriate level of care is provided for this problem. Specialist eating disorder assessments centre on eating difficulties, compensatory behaviours and the emotional impact of this on a day-to-day basis. If you look back at the assessments of both Niamh and Heidi, you will see that the following were covered in both:

- history of eating difficulties and/or behaviours

- body image

- developmental history (albeit in a limited capacity).

We are basically assessing whether this young person fits the criteria outlined in the *DSM-5* and *ICD-11* (American Psychiatric Association 2013; World Health Organization 2018) manuals for eating disorders, as described in Chapter 1. A range of questionnaires (often service-specific), including the EDE-Q (also discussed in Chapter 1), are completed by the young person and their family at the point of assessment. These will be routinely used throughout treatment to assess progress.

Because assessments are often structured, formalized and occasionally completed in a crisis situation (such as in Heidi's assessment), the context to the problem is often missed unless the practitioner feels skilled and confident enough to explore beyond the questions in the standardized assessment paperwork (Kinnaird *et al.* 2017), and this is where autism can be overlooked. Ruth shares how important this is:

> Getting to the root cause of the problem is important. I use mine [my eating disorder] to cope with change and situations that I feel out of control in. So, until I fix them, the eating disorder still comes in.
>
> *(Ruth)*

Symptomatology such as calorie counting, excessive exercise and regularly weighing can often look like an eating disorder at face value; however, these behaviours can also contribute to obsessional traits, whether number-based or an effective measure to reduce anxiety, which may be associated with autism. Practitioners in the eating disorder field are highly aware that individuals with AN also show features of autism (mostly social communication difficulties) that subside when they are re-nourished. This is cited heavily in the literature (Tchanturia *et al.* 2016, 2017). Clinical psychologist William Mandy makes the following observations:

I think one of the challenges that has really, sort of, I wouldn't say 'held back the field', but has really represented a significant challenge to clinicians and to researchers is that, actually, the psychological effects of starvation can mimic, in some ways, the characteristics of autism.

So, one of the real challenges has been, if you like, to discriminate between symptoms that actually arise from starvation and those that reflect, that truly reflect, an underlying autism spectrum disorder. And I think that's led people to miss autism amongst people who are experiencing anorexia because they, if you like, dismiss their social difficulties as merely the result, a kind of side effect, of their eating disorder. (Elliott and Mandy 2018)

There are, however, other means by which autism can be established or identified – that is, by looking at personal history and early development prior to the exacerbation of eating difficulties (as eating problems may have always been present but have only increased in severity). The eating disorder assessment should include early development, but time constraints and practitioner skill may hinder the detail of the information provided or how that information is obtained. You will have noticed that there was very little detail, if any, about Niamh's and Heidi's developmental history, so there is an incomplete picture of who these young people were prior to the problem developing. Consider Mandy's narrative (below) about Niamh's development. Does it change your clinical perspective of Niamh?

Niamh had always been an unusual, quirky child. She took a while to actually speak, but once she did you would never dream she was from the northwest of England. She had a beautiful speaking voice – people would often say, 'Where does she get that accent from?' We had no idea. At school the teachers would call her 'their shining star'.

She was clever and the first at the school to finish the reading scheme in Reception. But she struggled to play with other children. If she could be in charge of the game, then she would love to organize everything and come up with ideas – she would spend hours organizing but then never actually played the game. She would play alone in the playground, arranging leaves or reading a book. School didn't seem too concerned and told me she seemed quite happy as she was. But she did want friends; from an early age she would cry and say that she wanted 'a real friend' or 'a friend like me'. I would invite friends round for tea and she would be excited but then refuse to play with them. She would cry if she didn't get invited to a party but then spend the whole party crying if she *was* invited.

I remember talking to a homeopath and (ridiculous as it sounds) saying, 'I think my 3-year-old may have depression'. I knew something was going on – always.

In Year 4, a wonderful teacher recognized Niamh's difficulties and, for the first time, here was someone trying to help. We would meet weekly and tried strategies to help Niamh with socializing and friendships. The teacher did mention autism then (she had her suspicions), but we never took it any further. I only knew one child with autism and I didn't recognize any similarities, so I thought nothing more of it. Another teacher friend regularly used to say that there was something different about Niamh, but I always felt there wasn't enough to take it any further. She excelled at school and at dancing. If I could turn the clock back, I would go back to Year 4 and pursue the possibility that the teacher might be right.

As Niamh got older, she felt more that she didn't fit in. She would cry because other children called her weird. She found it hard to maintain friendships as she was brutally honest about everything (something as a family we love about her) and would comment inappropriately all the time, upsetting friends and family. At school she would refuse to do the work and do whatever she felt like instead. She would confidently state that her idea was better or that the work set was boring or pointless. Thankfully, despite this, she was liked by the teachers.

Looking back, Niamh has always been a perfectionist and she was no different when it came to her eating disorder. She continued to struggle. We tried a private psychologist for a while, but Niamh wouldn't talk to her.

(Mandy)

A richer and more holistic picture is established if you take this developmental information and combine it with a more curious position, as in Niamh's assessment in Chapter 2. For example, identifying and clarifying the following:

- Why did Niamh change her diet to vegetarianism and then veganism?

- The duration of entrenched thought – was it new or was it how Niamh had always thought?

- What was the nature of the rigidity of thought?

- Why did she not want to become fat?

- What was the function of the refusal to eat?

- Further exploration of what 'sensitive' meant, what the friendship difficulties were, and what was driving the worrying and perfectionism.

Knowing about these additional pointers, would you consider using them now to better inform the assessment process?

Do you think getting more of a perspective from an autism angle in your assessment would be helpful?

WHAT ABOUT CONTINUOUS ASSESSMENT?

Some services offer continuous assessment, but within the context of eating disorders this is rare due to staff capacity and service design. There are definitely benefits in a continuous assessment, especially in individuals where the context of their difficulties is multi-layered (i.e. more time is required in order to unpick the problem and establish a working formulation). Young people's familiarity with practitioners can prove to be both positive and negative: on the one hand, they may feel more comfortable sharing their difficulties; on the other hand, if the young person is not accepted by the service, this can be very disheartening and prevent the establishment of future trusting relationships. Identifying autism in a one-off assessment is very difficult, especially in girls who have been known to mask their difficulties (Fisher Bullivant 2018). It is a very difficult balance to strike. In my [Sharleen's] experience, being open and transparent with young people and their families about the purpose of a continuous assessment is often valued.

Dietetic assessment

Due to the increase in the number of young people with autism or suspected autism presenting to our eating disorder service, I [Sharleen] have changed my practice and now incorporate a detailed exploration of sensory aspects within my assessment. This includes interoception (helps us identify what is going on inside our body, such as hunger, thirst, feeling hot or cold), and taste, smell, visual/sight, auditory and tactile responses. I tend to not explore proprioception and vestibular processing (how we perceive the position and movement of our body) as these are unlikely to be related to dietary intake; however, they may still arise in questioning (sensory needs are explored in more detail in Chapter 5).

Hunger and fullness

I am often met with confused expressions when I start exploring hunger and fullness – it is an experience that a lot of us take for granted, but what if we never experience such cues, or it looks different to what we perceive it to be, or we are overly sensitive to the experience? This can be the case for people with the sensory processing difficulties that can accompany autism or ARFID.

It is not uncommon to meet young people who never feel hungry or thirsty and for whom eating/drinking becomes just 'another thing to do', requiring alarms or family members to continually remind them to eat. On the flip side, there are those who also never feel full, and guidance on portion-controlled meals is necessary. Admittedly, I have very little experience of the latter at eating disorder services as they usually present at weight-management services. It is not uncommon for people with restrictive eating to experience early satiety (feeling full quickly) and the gastrointestinal discomfort that accompanies this. However, there can be subtle differences. Those with heightened sensory needs are distressed at the physical process of 'eating' and 'feeling full'; but those who are not are often distressed as a result of the 'guilt' from consuming food, with feelings of fullness causing discomfort but not impacting their daily functioning. Indeed, both groups may report that they are 'feeling fat', but the context to this feeling is very different. There may also be subtle differences with regard to feeling hungry. Those with heightened sensory needs may feel distressed at the body's physical response to hunger, and often these young people will respond to this by eating (meeting their nutritional needs will then be offset by their early satiety). For those without heightened sensory needs, there is again more of an emotional response such as guilt, and sometimes even pleasure, as they persist with their restraint. This is not to say that such emotional responses do not occur for those with heightened sensory needs – they can do. It is important to distinguish whether there are any subtle differences within the assessment.

Mealtimes

It is important to evaluate the mealtime environment with regard to who is present, the level of activity (i.e. is it a noisy environment?) and where mealtimes occur (i.e. at a table or in front of the television). Mealtimes are usually a very distressing time for our young people and their families; there can often be a lot of arguing, crying and negotiating. Managing these times can often seem overwhelming.

> We couldn't get her out of the house for school, and breakfast was a battle. I would find her crouched in the porch, crying and shaking when I thought she had left for school.
>
> She had started to throw food at me in temper. She would hide food in her room, her bag, up her sleeve.
>
> — (Mandy)

It is very important to establish the context to the difficulties, as aspects such as sensory needs or lack of structure may cause undue distress for those with autism. For example, I had one young person who struggled with the noises at mealtimes (e.g. the chewing of others, the cutlery scraping the plate). This meant that she would become very distressed and would refuse to eat, leading to further noise as a result of arguments. This is very different to refusing to eat because of thoughts around weight and shape. This is not to say that thoughts about weight and shape will not be present, but they are minor players compared with the individual's relationship with their senses and/or sense of control. All mealtimes evoke sensory stimuli in the form of sight, sound and smell, and exploring each of these with the young people will provide a more rounded picture of their difficulties.

History of eating behaviours

Aspects such as feeding at birth and transitions are usually covered within the wider assessment. However, from a dietetic perspective, it is important to explore types of food, long-standing food avoidances and the context behind these – for example, are they sensory-related or associated with a previous trauma such as choking? As previously indicated, those who present with ARFID often have long-standing difficulties with food, and further restriction can be triggered in response to a particular event.

Relationship with food

Young people with eating disorders are described as having a poor relationship with food, and this can be evident in their need to calorie count, their avoidance of certain foods/drinks, and/or their need to meticulously examine food labels with regard to certain food groups. However, it is not unusual to see young people with eating disorders develop hobbies and interests around food, such as baking, cooking and watching TV cooking programmes, which appear to be in contrast to the illness itself. This is, in fact, not unusual. The effects of starvation often cause a preoccupation with food to develop (Kalm and Semba 2005), which usually resolves when the person is re-nourished. The difficulty arises when trying to distinguish between these 'preoccupations', and whether it is a special interest that has tipped into an obsession for those with autism. Establishing a timeline can be a helpful tool to distinguish between the two.

Weight and body image

Again, this should be covered within the wider assessment. However, it is essential we explore the young person's relationship with their weight and the processes around this. Not all young people have target weights and there can be subtle differences in why people want to lose weight. For example, a young person may want to lose weight in order to change their shape, whilst others (most likely with autism) may have no concerns regarding their weight and shape, preferring 'the number on the scales going down' or the security of the numbers and rules around food which feeds into their obsessive traits. This was the case for Ruth and Niamh, respectively:

> When unwell [I had] a feeling of having achieved something if the number had gone down. I think that where eating disorder treatment can fail [is when] it's all about the behaviours but doesn't always tackle the reasons behind them.
>
> —————— (Ruth)

> It wasn't about my body, or my weight. I wasn't scared of getting fat, I was scared of myself. Who was I without anorexia? Food was a quiet place in my mind – the numbers and the rules I made myself made me feel secure. But none of that really mattered. As much as the team helped, they weighed me each week and sent me away when I was physically healthy. I ate fine. I seemed fine. So what was the problem? I didn't know. So I agreed.
>
> —————— (Niamh)

For Heidi there was no preoccupation about the number on the scales and it was more about how she and others saw her, regardless of what her weight actually was – this was Heidi's attempt at fitting into a world where she felt different. These are important differences to establish.

Social media/internet usage

We currently live in an age of rapid technological advancement and it can feel difficult, if not sometimes overwhelming, to keep up with the latest app from one week to the next. However, internet usage and social media are largely how young people and their peers interact and feel connected, so it is necessary and important to assess the platforms they access. The mixture of visual media, such as Instagram and Facebook, and its spread of stereotypes among peers may be linked to an increased risk of eating concerns (Fardouly and Vartanian 2015; Smith, Hames and Joiner 2013; Syed-Abdul *et al.* 2013). It can be useful to redirect young people and their families to reliable sources of information, as well as to provide education as part of the therapeutic process.

NIAMH'S ASC AND THE MENTAL HEALTH ASSESSMENT PROCESS

Once Niamh was on the right pathway to address her individual needs, she had to go through yet more assessments. This assessment period spanned many months as we were trying to identify not only the difficulties she was having with her emotional well-being but also whether she had autism. It was also lengthy because it took time to build that therapeutic relationship with her as she had seen so many clinicians before and had had numerous assessments. Both Niamh and I [Fiona] worked hard on trying to understand the function/origin of her eating disorder, anxiety and low mood.

Together we identified:

- obsessional thinking

- inflexibility of thought

- social confusion

- difficulties with theory of mind

- difficulties with initiating maintaining and sustaining friendships and relationships

- executive functioning difficulties

- emotional dysregulation

- a significant discrepancy between Niamh's general cognitive ability and her ability to label, understand and express her emotions and those of others

- physical un-wellness, tiredness, feeling 'foggy' and overwhelmed.

Niamh and I together found a mutual understanding. This understanding was that I needed to listen to Niamh and be led by her rather than try to do things with her in the way I 'should' do them; to use my experience, skill and knowledge to guide my understanding of Niamh but most of all to really listen and watch her body language and adapt to her and what she was experiencing in the sessions with me; to know when to ease off and when to encourage. Niamh's mum was pivotal in these early stages as she was the interpreter between Niamh and me.

Earlier, I described Niamh's identified difficulties. What became apparent during this assessment period was that what was going to be helpful for Niamh was for me to name and explain the differences which were impacting on her and which were therefore resulting in difficulties for her. I would then need to enable Niamh to understand those differences and reframe the difficulties into differences so as to encourage a more positive slant on how she approached and managed those difficulties. By using appropriate strategies and interventions, but using them flexibly, I was seeking to guide Niamh to increase her understanding of self. For example, trying to explain emotions and get Niamh to label and identify them was not helpful, as what we found out after numerous sessions was that Niamh had a unique way of expressing herself. She used colours and shapes and mind mapping (e.g. diagrams) to describe and express how she interpreted her own emotions. This discovery gave me some insight into how differently Niamh was understanding and processing her emotions.

This then led on to more essential assessments (cognitive and sensory) to help me and Niamh understand her different thinking in order to implement the most effective interventions and strategies for Niamh to replicate and introduce into her life to help her manage her emotions in a more meaningful and appropriate way for her and those around her.

Investing in all this foundational assessment work gave me the knowledge to request further and additional specific assessments to assist the holistic picture we were beginning to gather on Niamh.

As well as the information gathering Niamh and I did, Niamh had started the process for the ASC assessment which is under NICE guidance:

> This guideline covers recognising and diagnosing autism spectrum disorder in children and young people from birth up to 19 years. It also covers referral. It aims to improve the experience of children, young people and those who care for them. (NICE 2017)

DEVELOPMENTAL HISTORY

The type and quality of developmental history that is obtained varies enormously. Unfortunately, in many clinical areas the information gathered is often inadequate, usually as a result of staff shortages, lack of commitment/funds for staff training and a general lack of understanding of the importance of offering a quality service. Too often in the field of autism we hear of, and experience, the cutting of corners in order to get through assessments and reduce waiting times. The impact can be catastrophic on the young person and their future, as significant elements of their difficulties can be missed if you are trying to observe, record and manage the young person's anxieties singlehandedly. Furthermore, reports often don't offer qualitative and significant evidence to support diagnosis and further clinical interventions.

Clinical measures

The following assessment tools may be used:

- *Autism Diagnostic Observation Schedule* (ADOS; Berument *et al.* 1999): This is a semi-structured autism observation measure and is the recognized gold standard for assessing autistic behaviour and diagnosing ASD across the age span, developmental levels and language skills. It requires extensive training and practice to administer and is usually conducted by psychologists or speech/language pathologists or specialist nurses in autism. In order to provide a quality and robust assessment, ADOS is best executed by two clinicians. If this is not available, then sound/video recording of the assessment is advisable and appropriate. There should be regular peer and supervised reliability checking; not only in the administration of the assessment but in the report writing.

- *Autism Diagnostic Interview – Revised* (ADI-R; Volkmar *et al.* 1994): This is a structured interview conducted with the parent/carer to obtain the developmental history and current behaviours. It focuses on the triad of impairments (social interaction, communication and imagination), but most clinicians have not had specific training in its use and some clinicians are so time-restricted in their clinics that they are unable to obtain a detailed, thorough history. Like the ADOS, the ADI requires extensive training and practice to administer and is usually conducted by a psychologist or speech/language pathologist or specialist nurse in autism.

- *Diagnostic Interview for Social and Communication Disorders* (DISCO; Brugha *et al.* 2012b): This is another structured interview and provides a holistic picture of the whole person through the story of their development and behaviour.

- *Childhood Autism Rating Scale, second edition* (CARS2; Schopler *et al.* 2010): This is a clinician-completed behaviour rating scale based on information gathered from two different forms (one is provided by parents/carers and the other by school).

- *Social Communication Questionnaire* (SCQ; Rutter, Bailey and Lord 2003): Formerly known as the Autism Screening Questionnaire (ASQ), this is a screening tool designed to identify children who may be on the autism spectrum. The SCQ was designed for use by parents/carers or the primary caregiver of children aged 4 years and over. The score identifies individuals who may be on the autism spectrum and who should be referred for a more complete assessment.

The SCQ questionnaire is given to parents/carers via school but since Niamh was home-educated this did not apply.

- *Questionnaire for Autism Spectrum Conditions (Q-ASC;* Attwood *et al.* 2011): This Autism Screening Questionnaire identifies behaviours and abilities consistent with the female presentation. If the results from the questionnaire are low but all the other parts of the assessment show evidence that is indicative of ASC, look at the patterns of the answers. There is often vital information in relation to the triad of impairments to scaffold the other evidence, and although it may not be enough for a diagnosis, it may lead to better understanding of the individual and be a guide for future assessments. We [Sharleen's children and young people's eating disorder team] are currently implementing the introduction of the Q-ASC at our young people's initial assessment with the eating disorder team, alongside their other screening/assessment tools. We are aware that this has to be done sensitively as some of the young people and their families have no inkling that ASC may be a factor. However, given current statistics indicating a high prevalence of autism with eating disorders (see Chapter 1), it is imperative that this be done at this stage. When there is evidence that it may be a factor, the autism specialist needs to be included in the MDT appointments with the family.

Home and school observations

From my [Fiona's] experience, school and home observations are essential to build a wider picture of the individual. Currently, because of time and cost, these observations are being discouraged and stopped. For me as a clinician, observing children and young people in all settings – both those where they feel comfortable and those where they feel not so comfortable – and watching how and when they interact gives an overall richer and more individualized understanding of what is happening for that young person. This can only lead to a more evidence-based outcome of diagnosis.

In summary, the assessments/measures continue to need the

framework of the current questions etc., but with the clinician's understanding and skill to look out of the box and gather more information in other meaningful ways and to interpret behaviours and clinical presentation in an informed evidence-based way with an up-to-date understanding of autism and in collaboration with individuals with autism.

It's also imperative that when we are conducting these interviews/ observations and questionnaires, we acknowledge that within the spectrum there is the further complexity of young people who mask (this occurs especially in young women, but we are becoming increasingly aware of young men who mask too).

Sensory responses

Unusual sensory responses are relatively common in children with autism spectrum disorder (ASD). Sensory issues are now included in the *DSM-5* (American Psychiatric Association 2013) ASD symptom criteria for restricted, repetitive patterns of behaviour, interests or activities, and include hyper-or hypo-reactivity to sensory input or unusual interest in sensory aspects of the environment, such as apparent indifference to pain/heat/cold, adverse response to specific sounds or textures, excessive smelling or touching of objects. As already indicated, this should be included as part of the assessment when exploring eating difficulties, and this will be examined further in Chapter 5.

Cognitive assessments

What has become evident in my [Fiona] work with this group of young people is the importance of knowing how they learn, process, plan, interpret and implement. This can be informed by cognitive assessments. The aim of having these assessments is not to obtain an IQ but to understand different thinking in order to inform therapy/ treatment interventions and enable the individual to understand how they function, in a more helpful and meaningful way.

CONCERNS AROUND ASSESSMENTS

There are numerous general measures which are used by different professional bodies, and other screening tools, but my [Fiona] concerns as a practitioner still involved in the assessment process are:

- Is the administration of the measures, information gathering and interpretation of the results from the clinician monitored and supervised?

- Is reliability checking implemented into the assessment process as good and essential practice?

- Is appropriate training being offered and undertaken by clinicians in order to ensure the information gathered is as accurate as possible and a gold standard assessment is actually administered?

- Are the forms explained to the reporters and are reasonable adjustments made for the reporters to get their information across in the most helpful and accurate way to represent the behaviours and difficulties of the individual?

- Are the results fed back to the individual and their parents/carers in an empathic, helpful manner so as to ensure positivity regarding diagnosis?

The power of the assessment should not be underestimated. As you can see from Niamh's journey, the psychologist that she met at her eating disorder assessment was the most valued person in her recovery. Families presenting at eating disorder services have often exhausted all of their resources in order to feed their child and are desperate to be listened to and have their concerns acknowledged. Indeed, a comprehensive assessment process itself can be very therapeutic for the young person and their family, instigating conversations and change. It is helpful to view the assessment process as ongoing, always in need of revisiting and reviewing, as we are always learning new things about the young people we work with.

If autism is already present at the time of the assessment, then consideration is required with regard to adaptation and alteration in format. If autism has not yet been identified, it should be explored as a possibility. This leads us to exploring current processes that are in place in CAMHS which help identify or assess autism and eating disorders. By doing so, we open up an opportunity that will inform us of what needs to be modified, changed and transformed.

CHAPTER 4

Identification and Formulation

IDENTIFICATION

It's important initially to focus on what it is we see in our clinical practice which makes us query autism in the young people who present at eating disorder services. Appropriate identification may contribute to the context of why a young person is experiencing eating difficulties. Autism was identified at different stages for Niamh (after her journey with eating disorder services) and Heidi (during her time with eating disorder services). Below are reflections on practitioner changes of practice with regard to Niamh and Heidi within the eating disorder service and how having access to those skilled and knowledgeable about autism opens opportunities for a different style of working and thinking.

REFLECTIONS ON CLINICAL PRACTICE

NIAMH

Autism was not considered when Niamh was under the eating disorder team. It is helpful to look back and question how we missed it. There are several reasons (from a personal perspective).

Lack of training

Autism alongside eating difficulties was not on the teaching curriculum when I [Sharleen] was in training. In fact, eating disorders were only briefly mentioned, therefore I was in the dark. From conversations with other health care professionals, this also appears to be the case for them. This is in no way a criticism, but practitioners default to what they know. It is much easier to label someone with anxiety, depression or an eating disorder (because then we know what to do, i.e. we can fit them in a box), rather than to think flexibly and adapt practice, which may involve exploring different avenues for some time. (Service and culture change are further explored in Chapter 8.)

Lack of experience

My [Sharleen's] previous work with autism was as a general paediatric dietitian where children would present with selective eating but grow and develop normally, or they had additional needs and were fed artificially. I would see these children for only 20–30 minutes every 4 months owing to the lack of paediatric dietitians and the service structure. I therefore felt my impact was minimal and inadequate (and if I am honest, I didn't know how to make a difference). This feeling is shared by other paediatric dietitians working in this field:

> I struggle with how to support them [young people and/or parents/ carers] to accept that food intake may not change for a long time and thus how to help them manage the negative emotions.
>
> Another main worry of mine, personally, is that there is such limited evidence around the strategies...as in all areas of nutrition, there is a lack of success with these strategies. Is that due to a lack of constant, persistent application of the strategies or perhaps because they simply just don't work? It's difficult to tell families 'to keep going' if the plan is never going to work. What does that feel like for them?
>
> *(Lisa, Community Paediatric Dietitian/Team Leader)*

> Overcoming food aversions in children with autism can feel like an uphill climb. I have great admiration for how these families cope on a day-to-day basis.
>
> *(Sophie, Specialist Paediatric Dietitian)*

I was also new to the field of eating disorders – in fact, Niamh was one of the first young people I saw with an eating disorder. Being new did, however, help me in one respect: I am very much a holistic and patient-centred dietitian and although I knew various literature had talked about questioning the choice of vegetarianism and veganism, I was not married to the idea and went with the request by Niamh and her mum for Niamh to be vegan. Although it was a risk, and admittedly I did have a 'What have I just done?' moment, I sensed the difference in the room and the need to maintain a therapeutic relationship with Niamh in order to promote recovery. However, at that time I did not know what that difference was.

Starvation can present like autism
The literature indicates that autistic traits such as obsessionality, rigidity and a seeming lack of empathy are heightened in those with starvation but that these traits resolve when the individuals are re-nourished (Pellicano and Hiller 2013). This makes formulation very difficult.

Eating disorders and generic CAMHS (where Fiona sits) were very separate
This means there is no cross-pollination of skills or knowledge. How can we understand what we don't yet know?

Lessons learnt and what to look out for
Reflection on Niamh's time with the eating disorder team may have been very different if we had explored the questions and reflections posed in Chapters 2 and 3. A more detailed investigation of the following may have led to an earlier identification of Niamh's autism:

- Evaluation of who Niamh was prior to the 'problem' – friendship problems were identified, and Niamh was described as self-critical, a worrier and a perfectionist, but these things were not explored further.

- Niamh's transition period to high school required further

exploration as her relationship with food altered significantly at this point.

- Her food rules and routines – their function and purpose.

- Body image – there was a lot of confusion for Niamh around this at assessment, but we now know it was never about weight or shape.

- Developmental history – obtaining more detail on why she was described as an 'odd' toddler, and her struggle with making and maintaining friendships.

- Her preference for short clinical sessions and not being able to connect with the emotional work.

- Niamh's affect and how she used verbal and body language to communicate (e.g. her accent and lack of gestures).

- The reasons for Niamh wanting to be home-schooled as this was related to social rather than academic aspects.

It was during Niamh's second episode of care with CAMHS that autism was identified.

Emilie, a senior nurse practitioner, shares the subtle signs Niamh exhibited that informed her of the possibility that Niamh might have autism:

When I was completing Niamh's assessment, I noticed subtle indications of possible autism.

Firstly, she spoke very well and with a slight accent that would not be expected from the area where she was born. The way she held and presented herself was as if I was having a conversation with someone much older. I often had to remind myself that she was only 14.

The way she talked about emotions was very visual; instead of usual typical language such as anxious or sad, she would describe feeling anxious as feeling like she was floating and the feeling of sadness as all-encompassing grey. Despite being academically outstanding, she referred to feelings of anxiety as 'paranoia' and was often unable to distinguish between the two.

I was also struck by the difficulties Niamh was experiencing in relation to socializing with people her own age. She often spoke about putting on an act and how draining she found socializing.

At this initial assessment, I discussed possible autistic traits with Niamh and her mum, and both were struck by how many were relatable to Niamh. I remember going back and forth as to whether I should discuss this with them as it had never been presented to them previously; however, the immediate positive reaction both Niamh and her mum had in response to our discussion proved it was absolutely the right thing to do.

HEIDI

As already mentioned, it was in joint dietetic and family sessions and through conversations on observations and behaviours by parents that autism was suspected.

> As the tension subsided and it seemed more possible for Heidi and her parents to get back to how things were, they were noticing how much Heidi was struggling to relate to people around her and how this led to her behaving in ways that could be described as anxious, depressed or eating disordered. Heidi's parents had also thought this might be normal teenage behaviour and weren't sure if this was to do with the illness or something else.
>
> — *(Sam, Family Therapist)*

Evidence building

I [Sharleen] remember when I initially joined family therapy sessions, Heidi preferred it if her sessions were always in the same room and Sam and I sat in the same place. We share our building with a number of mental health teams and therefore there was often a lot of negotiation to ensure that we had this room, and we were not always successful. This caused Heidi a lot of anxiety. When I met Heidi outside of the therapy room setting – for example, if we met in the corridor when she was seeing the consultant psychiatrist – she would not communicate with me or even acknowledge me. When discussing emotions or relationships (core work within eating disorders), Heidi became frustrated and didn't engage, often reporting that practitioners weren't listening to her. Sam and I found ourselves changing therapeutic tack in order to maintain our relationship with Heidi, and this was often outside the manualized approach to eating disorders.

Seeking consultation regarding autism

We [Sam and Sharleen] were highly aware of taking an alternative approach with this young person, but it also felt like we were groping in the dark for what we could do or say next that would be useful in Heidi's care. Based on our session observations, as well as reports from Heidi and her family about her communication and friendship difficulties, we suspected autism but we were very conscious that we were not specialists in this area. We therefore approached Fiona for consultation on how best to work with this young person. We then shared our formulation with Heidi and her parents, and for them it finally made sense. We gained their consent to refer Heidi to the ASC pathway.

Led by the young person

Like Niamh, when Heidi expressed the desire to transition to solid food, she outlined that it would be on her terms (as discussed in Chapter 6) with support from her family and the team as and when needed. Because of what had been observed to date, the trust that we [Sam and Sharleen] had established and the current 'stuck' position we found ourselves in (in terms of feeding), we acknowledged and supported Heidi to take the lead but we also made an agreement with her that we would need to intervene if we saw deterioration in her mental or physical health.

Sensory difficulties

Through Fiona's guidance, Heidi's relationship with numbers was explored. She found comfort in calorie counting as it ensured she was 'getting enough'; however, she acknowledged that she didn't like it when her calorie intake had to increase as this would affect her not only in terms of her routine but also on a sensory level. She was able to share how uncomfortable feelings of fullness were for her and how she struggled to understand why other people were trying to 'force' her to eat more when she was having such a strong physical sensation not to (often resulting in involuntary vomiting). The liquid diet was more tolerable on a sensory level. Heidi reported that the number on the scales did not bother her but she did struggle with how she saw herself – she felt different and just wanted to be normal. Weight loss had led to people initially making positive comments about her shape and size instead of the previous negative ones. However, this shifted again when she became 'too thin'. This caused Heidi considerable confusion.

Fiona's perspective on identifying autism in those with eating disorders

It is not usually the case that eating difficulties are highlighted on assessment of autism – if they are, it is usually within the context of obsessional thinking/behaviour that is sensory- and/or anxiety-led. It is during the 'getting to know' period with the young person and their families that eating difficulties become more apparent, in which case I will have become increasingly aware and concerned that I am unable to influence positive change with the individual by using my usual strategies and interventions. I would then seek preventative not reactive advice from my colleagues in the Community Eating Disorder Service (CEDS).

When I am approached by CEDS for a consultation about one of the young people they are seeing, the thing I notice most when I listen to the clinicians is that they have identified that their interventions are not working. By that I mean their young people are struggling to understand or implement what is being asked of them, or the clinicians are having difficulty communicating to them what they need them to do, or the young people are having difficulty expressing their difficulties in a way the clinicians understand. The way the clinicians describe their young people will often mirror the difficulties of the young people themselves. Their communication styles are often different: the young people are described as direct and very forthright, introverted and lacking in affect. They may be high achievers and perfectionists in education, sports and the arts but then struggle with initiating, maintaining and sustaining friendships. They are often very articulate when talking about their interests and studies, but when challenged emotionally they find it difficult to identify, process and express their own and others' emotions, losing that ability to articulate.

When I meet these young people, I can often quite quickly see their social awkwardness, their frustration at not being able to identify and express emotions, their confusion about why they are experiencing difficulties with eating and also why those around them are worried about them.

It is often helpful to identify that the function/reason/origin of the eating difficulty is not about image or weight but more to do with obsessional thinking, a sensory issue or anxiety. Milton (2012) talks about a hypersensitivity to sensations of external events, and hyposensitivities with internal feelings. Initially it is helpful to recommend taking a developmental history from parents/carers, incorporating questions about whether there is a need to parent differently between siblings, and whether there are social anxieties, difficulties with friendships, obsessional traits and sensory processing difficulties. A timeline of when eating became different is often helpful as this can identify ongoing difficulties in eating or a more recent onset of an eating disorder. Shea (2015) writes:

Food neophobia – Between the ages of 18–24 months food refusal generally becomes more prominent. Neophobia (fear of the new) is a typical stage in the development of food acceptance whereby children reject foods if they haven't seen others eat them first. This is an adaptive response, protecting children, once they are independently mobile, from eating anything potentially unsafe. Typically, neophobia dissipates with:

- age

- the imitation of others eating

- the development of cognitive categories.

However, the social and cognitive difficulties in autistic people mean that neophobia persists for much longer with the ongoing rejection of new or perceptually dissimilar foods.

One would then offer a consultation with the young person. Often, written information does not give you the flavour of that individual – it is only by meeting with them that you can observe qualities/ difficulties within an interaction. The focus here is to monitor their eye contact: can they modulate their eye contact? Does it change when they are talking about interests and motivators? Does it change when you focus on identifying their own and others' emotions, their understanding of their own and others' emotions and how they manage both? In addition, is there reciprocity in the conversation, even when talking about the things they prefer to talk about? Can they demonstrate theory of mind? What is their affect like? Can you read them facially and by their body language? How flexible are their thoughts and behaviours? Are they obsessional and what does that look like? If they are perfectionists, where does that originate – is it systemic or does it come from inflexibility of thought? Take a history of how they manage friendships and relationships in general. It's important to look at this history as the average age of young people being assessed is 14–16, by which time young people may have learnt how to appear to be managing relationships, or mimic or mask. It's crucial to get information from teachers' and parents'/carers' perspectives in this area, because if the young person has difficulty acknowledging, understanding and expressing their experiences of relationships and difficulties with understanding how others see them, you may not get an accurate picture.

One would request an educational/clinical psychology assessment, particularly around executive function and style of learning and processing. Sometimes, if the young person is on the autistic spectrum, they may for example score highly in memory, word recognition and spelling but may struggle with the comprehension elements of literacy due to their lack of understanding of subtext and social clues. According to Starlight and Stories (2014): 'If a student is struggling to understand relationship conventions in real life, they will also struggle to interest [sic] how conventions are being broken down or upheld in text.'

A person with autism often has a spiky or uneven profile of abilities and capacities. For example, they may be good at reading but their processing may be significantly different. Individuals who are very eloquent verbally are often incorrectly assumed to be capable in areas in which they genuinely struggle.

Difficulties in the way the brain processes information are also documented in autistic people and can help to explain features of their diet. For example, cognitive rigidity and the 'desire for sameness' may result in an adherence to particular routines or rituals around food, such as having to have the same utensils, with context often being the first predictor of whether a food is safe.

After gathering all this information, one would formulate the evidence and share it with the CEDS team in order to inform the most appropriate way forward therapeutically for the young person.

One would look holistically to inform formulation, including the strengths and qualities of the young person as well as the things they experience difficulties with.

FORMULATION

Johnstone (2012) describes formulation as 'the process of making sense of a person's difficulties in the context of their relationships, social circumstances, life events, and the sense they have made of them.'

As a dietitian entering the clinical field of mental health, I [Sharleen] remember the first time I heard the word 'formulation'. Being from a scientific background, I thought, 'What has maths got to do with it?' I can now look back and laugh at my naïvety. Dietitians do formulate in their practice, but their formulation is different from that of mathematicians, in that the terminology is often more medicalized and structured. This means it often takes the label of 'diagnosis', which takes an expert position (and an expert position provides safety). Unsurprisingly, many non-mental health care professionals struggle with their understanding of formulation. It is important we use language or define the concepts we are discussing, not only with our young people but also with our wider professional team.

There are various theoretical models on formulation which provide structure and direction. Some of these are specific to each therapy field. Indeed, working within the eating disorder MDT means that the various professions will formulate the problem from different perspectives. Such models can guide the practitioner in their questioning but they can also prevent further exploration of the information provided. If we look back at Niamh's time within the eating disorder service (see Chapter 3), she reported difficulties with friendships, her body image and difficulties transitioning; however, it is difficult to provide a formulation as the context of these difficulties was not fully explored. The perceived problem – dietary restriction – was seen only for what it was and therefore the intervention targeted that problem. What wasn't seen at that time was that the dietary restriction was a symptom of the wider difficulties that Niamh was experiencing in terms of her undiagnosed autism. This collaborative formulation was made later on in her journey (under general CAMHS services) through acknowledgement of:

- difficulties with her cognitive style and how she understood and processed information

- sensory processing difficulties which were impacting on her emotional state and how she was able to access her community

- a significant discrepancy between general cognitive ability and emotional connection and expression

- emotional dysregulation

- difficulties in how she expressed and described her emotions

- a significant impact from social and generalized anxiety on her physical state and well-being

- her literal way of expressing and understanding language and her sometimes lack of reciprocity

- Niamh's reflection where she explained that the function/ origin of her eating disorder was not around body image but around control of overwhelming emotions and wanting to be vegan.

So why is the context to the problem often not explored? Often, practitioners default to what they know, and this is understandable. However, difficulties arise when traditional methods of working are ineffective and there is a consequential detriment to the young person's physical health. This causes anxiety not only for the young person and their parents/carers but also for the practitioner. Increasingly, we see children and young people being passed around services because they are 'refusing to eat'. By the time they reach the eating disorder team, they are at crisis point and there is also no evidence of formulation or context to the problem.

Indeed, formulation is fluid and not rigid, and it is important to acknowledge this. As we gather more information through the therapeutic relationship with both the young person and their family, our formulation may change. This can be demonstrated in Heidi's case.

HEIDI
Formulation at presentation

Heidi was diagnosed with atypical anorexia nervosa and a depressive disorder. It was difficult to formulate her problems at the time of assessment on account of the physical crisis she presented with.

Heidi appeared to be unhappy with her body image and developed concerns regarding healthy eating after a talk at school (acting as a trigger). There was also difficulty with friendships that may have contributed to her unhappiness. This led to Heidi restricting her eating and a subsequent significant weight loss.

After inpatient stay and follow-up community sessions

Heidi's eating difficulties can be explained in the context of her autism. Social communication difficulties led to her feeling isolated and anxious with an innate feeling of being 'different' and an 'outsider'. This significantly impacted friendships, especially when she started high school. A healthy eating talk at school triggered an interest/ obsession which resulted in weight loss (which was never Heidi's purpose); however, this subsequently led to Heidi receiving positive comments instead of the previous perceived negative comments from people (affecting her sense of 'fitting in'). Heidi's obsessionality around numbers (in terms of calorie counting) provided a soothing effect for her anxiety and gave her something to focus on. Heidi's 'healthy' eating led to reduced portion sizes, which then triggered her senses in terms of fullness. Her rigid routine around food and early satiety meant that she struggled to increase her intake.

SUMMARY OF LESSONS LEARNED

Gathering and identifying the correct information from a wide range of sources will strongly inform a psychological formulation, ensuring that appropriate care and treatment is provided by the most relevant services. This is where the initial assessment process, as detailed in Chapter 3, becomes very important, laying the foundations for a young person's journey of care. Therefore, if autism is suspected, identified or is already present, we must not rule out further co-morbidities, considerations and risk (physical and mental). We will cover this aspect in the next chapter.

CHAPTER 5

Co-morbidities, Considerations and Risk

To further add to the complexity of eating disorders and autism in young people, it is not unusual for other mental health conditions to be at play. This chapter provides insight into the co-morbidities most commonly seen in this cohort and describes the risk associated with such presentations. In addition, the chapter covers aspects that are not necessarily 'diagnosable' but which need to be considered clinically as they have an impact on daily functioning and impact on how we work therapeutically.

CO-MORBIDITIES
Depression
The *DSM-5* (American Psychiatric Association 2013) states that an individual must have a two-week period of experiencing at least five of the following, where one of the symptoms should be anhedonia (loss of interest or pleasure) or depressed mood:

- significant weight loss due to lack of appetite

- depressed mood throughout the whole day, as well as daily

- anhedonia

- delayed thought and movement

- lethargy and lack of energy daily

- not feeling worthy

- inability to concentrate

- thoughts of death and attempting to end their life.

To receive a diagnosis of depression, these symptoms must cause the individual clinically significant distress or impairment in social, occupational or other important areas of functioning. The symptoms must also not be a result of substance abuse or another medical condition.

When Heidi presented to the eating disorder service, she was also diagnosed with depression. It is not unusual to see low mood in those with eating disorders as it is a side effect of malnutrition. However, based on the timeline Heidi reported, it was believed that her depression was present for some time before she began engaging in restricted eating. This was triggered by how she felt about herself and fragmented relationships with friends, which we now know is in the context of her autism and 'feeling different'. Addressing eating difficulties and restriction can be particularly difficult when a young person is depressed, therefore it is important that this is acknowledged so that intervention is appropriately tailored.

Anxiety

The *DSM-5* (American Psychiatric Association 2013) includes a range of anxiety disorders, including separation anxiety disorder, selective mutism, social anxiety disorder, and generalized anxiety and panic disorder. Anxiety is often observed in those with eating disorders. Initially it can be difficult to determine whether it is occurring in the context of the eating disorder or whether it is a separate mental health condition. For those who present with restrictive eating, the cause of their anxiety can usually be deciphered when they become well-nourished, and the anxiety is often observed moving to another area of their life.

REFLECTIONS ON CO-MORBIDITIES

NIAMH

Alongside her diagnoses of autism and an eating disorder, Niamh now also has a diagnosis of generalized and social anxiety disorder.

> She was sad, anxious and struggling with things that had never been a problem before. Ballet had always been her happy place, and suddenly we were having to coax her in after sitting in the car, tearful and angry, for half an hour. Niamh had become very attached to me. She would climb into bed with me and even wanted me in the bathroom when she was having a bath. She would link me all the time or hold my hand. I was worried this would never end. Niamh started to research what was wrong with her. By the time we got to see the GP again she had diagnosed herself with anxiety, depression and bi-polar disorder. She had reached rock-bottom. Although she looked physically healthier, she was worse than ever. She didn't want to go back to CAMHS (and neither did I) but she felt she needed medicating and I thought it was worth a try. Her main focus each day was to survive the day. At that point I was scared she might attempt suicide. She seemed to hate herself. She was so isolated – school had become impossible, so she was at home with me most of the time. She did have a few friends but kept them at a distance. I feel so thankful that the referral from our GP brought us to Emilie.
>
> — *(Mandy)*

Given the information from Niamh's developmental history and the knowledge I [Fiona] have from working with her, it appears that her social anxiety stemmed from the autism and then fed into the generalized anxiety. Niamh struggled with her mood and anxiety for many years and it was impacting on her everyday functioning. As previously described, the referral back into CAMHS from the GP detailed many of the criteria listed above. Niamh now takes the antidepressant sertraline and has reported significant benefits in addition to those she has gained from engaging in therapeutic work.

Ehlers-Danos Syndrome (EDS)

The *DSM-5* (American Psychiatric Association 2013) states that EDS is a group of rare inherited conditions that affect connective tissue. Connective tissues provide support in skin, tendons, ligaments, blood vessels, internal organs and bones. There are several types of EDS that may share some symptoms. These include an increased range of joint movement (joint hypermobility), stretchy skin, and fragile skin that breaks or bruises easily.

I [Fiona] am currently working with numerous young people who have an additional diagnosis of EDS, and many of them experience the multiple features of EDS. (Some of these young people's mothers have an EDS diagnosis, too.)

Obsessive compulsive disorder (OCD)

The *DSM-5* (American Psychiatric Association 2013) defines OCD as the presence of obsessions, compulsions, or both, which are time consuming (take more than one hour per day), are not attributable to the physiological effects of a substance and are not better explained by the symptoms of another mental health condition.

Diagnosing OCD in those with autism can prove difficult as OCD rituals can often resemble the repetitive behaviours common in autism, and vice versa. However, from clinical experience, I [Fiona] have often observed those with eating disorders and autism also having OCD. The important difference is often the purpose or motivation of the obsessions and compulsions: those with OCD perform something ritualistic because they believe something bad is going to happen to them, whereas in those with autism it is an innate way of being.

OTHER CONSIDERATIONS
Sensory needs

As already indicated in Chapter 3, exploring the senses should be a routine part of assessment. Sensory information is not just limited to the traditional five senses: sight (visual), smell, taste, touch (tactile) and sound (auditory); it also includes:

- *Interoception:* The perception of sensations inside the body (e.g. hunger and fullness).

- *Proprioception:* The sense of self movement and body position.

- *Vestibular processing:* This includes the part of the inner ear and brain that help control balance, eye movement and spatial awareness.

For the majority of us, effective sensory integration ('making sense' of the world around us) occurs automatically. However, there are those for whom the process demands effort and attention, with no guarantee of accuracy; they are oversensitive to sensory input, undersensitive, or both. These sensory difficulties may, but not always, accompany autism and may be a trigger for ARFID.

The majority of senses impact not only the process of eating but also the digestive process itself. Have you ever stopped and taken note of what you do when you try a new food? Often people take longer to look at it, they smell it, they are wary of that first taste, and they pay attention to how they feel after they have eaten it – this is utilizing the senses to gauge the safety of the food and whether to have it again. In individuals who are oversensitive to their senses these 'feelings' can be overwhelming and lead to meltdowns. For example, Heidi described in her assessment how she struggled with never feeling hungry ('Why would I eat when I am just not hungry?'). When she did eat, she experienced fullness and what was deemed as purging by family members. However, further exploration of Heidi's world revealed that the 'purging' was actually an involuntary sensory response to feeling too full. It was this oversensitivity that meant Heidi was only tolerating liquids at discharge from the SEDU. Exploring the context behind these behaviours is vital in order to provide appropriate therapeutic intervention.

Environment

The spaces in which we see young people need to be considered. For example, Heidi preferred a particular therapy room – it was smaller than our other spaces and it was important that we sat in the same places at each session. This provided safety for Heidi. CAMHS and NHS buildings are often not very autism-friendly – they are busy places, with lots of conflicting noises. Service capacity often means that home visits cannot be facilitated; however, these can make all the difference for the young person with autism:

> I remember trying to encourage a boy to come into the health centre, but he was highly distressed – kicking and screaming because he did not want to come in. I changed tack and saw him at his home – I sat in his tent with him and he was really calm. (Heather, Specialist Community Dietitian)

When physical health has not been compromised, I [Sharleen], like Fiona, have taken my dietetic sessions outdoors – for some, a walk in a park or in nature provides a more relaxed space to talk and engage. It can also be helpful to allow pets into sessions as they are often a means of reducing anxiety in an environment that is emotionally overwhelming and exhausting.

School provision

Because of the physical consequences of eating disorders, especially those that are restrictive in nature, it may be necessary to withdraw from school or college attendance. This can be a difficult decision as education is often a welcome distraction, provides structure to the day, and is a motivator for the young person. However, these benefits need to be balanced with the young person's health. School/college is an environment that causes physical and emotional exertion and it is often in the best interests of the young person to withdraw for a period of time so that they can focus on attaining a better-nourished state. Liaison with the education system is vital during this time as there are often options available to ensure that the young person does not fall behind academically.

Sleep difficulties

Sleep difficulties are common amongst those with eating disorders and those with autism, independently. Evidence shows that starvation induces waking in order to seek out food and nourishment. As a dietitian, I often ask about sleep – for those who are no longer receiving hunger signals, it can be a useful mechanism to explore how else the body is seeking out food and responding to starvation (e.g. waking frequently in the night, taking frequent naps during the day).

RISK

People with eating disorders – in particular those with AN – are high-risk in terms of their own health and safety. The factors involved in the assessment of risk in people with eating disorders are described below.

Physical or medical health

> She became very ill, very quickly. She was tired and lethargic and cold all the time. She had a big coat with a hood that she wore all the time; I grew to hate it with a passion.
>
> *(Mandy)*

Assessing, identifying and managing physical risk form a significant part of eating disorder management and it is beyond the scope of this book to cover all aspects. However, it is important to highlight the main areas in order to increase awareness. The physical/medical risk arises from a combination of the restrictive behaviours (food and sometimes fluid) and the compensatory behaviours. Features in the person's history that indicate medical risk are:

- excess exercise with low weight

- blood in vomit

- inadequate fluid intake in combination with poor eating

- rapid weight loss

- factors that disrupt ritualized eating habits (e.g. holidays or exams).

Screening of the above parameters will indicate the need for physical stabilization on a paediatric ward (further described in Chapter 6) and the management of refeeding syndrome. Refeeding syndrome is defined as potentially fatal shifts in fluids and electrolytes that may occur in malnourished people receiving intensive refeeding (Mehanna, Moledina and Travis 2008). Although this is extremely rare, it is important to minimize the risk of it occurring.

Young people may report the following physical symptoms (their number, frequency and duration will inform the clinical assessment):

- dizziness

- headaches

- chest pain

- cramping

- hair changes – becomes thin and brittle, lanugo hair (soft, downy hair)

- skin changes – colour, dryness, broken skin, pressure sores, poor healing

- gastrointestinal changes

- oedema (fluid retention)

- blackouts

- fainting

- fits

- feeling cold (especially hands and feet)

- blue lips/dry lips

- reflux

- swollen parotid glands

- loss of or irregular menstruation in females

- pins and needles

- dental problems

- lethargy/fatigue.

It is routine to regularly complete bloods, electrocardiogram (ECG), muscle strength test, blood pressure, pulse rate, core temperature and peripheral circulation observations. From my clinical experience, the completion of routine physical observations can be distressing for those with heightened sensory responses. It is important to establish whether they feel more comfortable with a particular health care professional (e.g. someone they are more familiar with, such as their GP).

It is important to point out that no single symptom mentioned is a good indicator of overall risk or illness. A robust risk assessment combines experienced clinical assessment with investigations, assessment of motivation and engagement with treatment plans, and available parent/carer support (Nicholls 2012).

Self-harm

The *DSM-5* (American Psychiatric Association 2013) describes self-harm or self-injury as being characterized by a deliberate and direct injury or damage of body tissue, usually intended without suicidal ideation. Arguably, eating disorders themselves can be seen as a form of self-harm in its broadest sense as they harm both health and the body. Self-harm commonly occurs in autism (Duerden *et al.* 2012) and eating disorders (Svirko and Hawton 2007) independently, and so we should be conscious that it occurrs in those with the dual diagnosis.

Establishing the underlying function of self-harming in those with both eating disorder and autism is important. Often its function is a means of escape, avoidance or regulation of aversive emotional states (Buckholdt *et al.* 2015). This was the case for Niamh:

> She would scratch her skin on her hands till it was raw and burn herself with straighteners.
>
> ———————————————— *(Mandy)*

However, in those with autism it may be useful to also consider atypical sensory processing and the need for sameness (Duerden et al. 2012).

Suicidal ideation

As already indicated, eating disorders have the highest mortality amongst all psychiatric illnesses (Arcelus et al. 2011), with suicide impacting on this rate. As well as the effect of malnutrition on the brain in terms of mood, eating disorders can feel exhausting and hopeless. We do not know the prevalence of suicide or suicidal thoughts in those with both autism and eating disorders; however, we need to be mindful that the complexities of both may increase the risk.

Heidi's engagement in self-harm was a communication of significant distress, coping with high levels of anxiety and being different. Combined with her depression, this led to Heidi also having suicidal thoughts. CBT and relaxation/mindfulness techniques were helpful for Heidi in managing this, as was communicating her needs and thoughts to her family. CBT may not always be the most effective measure to address co-morbidities as it very much depends on presentation and formulation. Chapter 6 covers various interventions and therapy modalities.

Risk, either physical or psychological, or both, may be the reason why young people and their families present to services such as CAMHS or CEDS. Within the eating disorder service, young people with autism often present to services in physical health crisis as their decision to alter their eating habits is instant, which leads to rapid and significant weight loss. They may or may not present in mental health crisis also. It is important to establish whether this risk can be managed or whether an admission is required to a paediatric ward and/or specialist inpatient care. This is covered in more detail in Chapter 6.

There are many other mental health conditions that have not been covered in this chapter, as well as matters such as gender identity. This is not to say that they do not occur in those who are experiencing eating disorders and autism but in my clinical experience they occur less frequently than those already discussed. As practitioners working in the field of mental health, we should always be aware that the young person before us could be affected by any kind of mental health condition(s) and/or gender identity issue(s).

CHAPTER 6

Therapy and Interventions

We have established that independent autism and eating disorders are assessed and identified using methods that are completely in contrast to each other. Unsurprisingly, this continues in terms of the therapeutic approaches and interventions recommended to treat and manage each of these complex clinical areas. In both our specialities we use family therapy/systemic work, but apart from that our therapeutic work and practical interventions differ significantly. Therapies and interventions need to be appropriate, meaningful and helpful.

AUTISM
Therapeutic interventions
To ensure delivery of the right intervention in an individualized way, start by exploring and trying to identify the function of a behaviour. In an ideal world, this would take the form of a functional analysis (LaVigna and Willis 1995). In addition, it is important to look at communication and the cognitive profile, and to identify any sensory issues.

In terms of the actual interventions, use combinations/variations and degrees of the following:

- a *very* flexible form of behavioural CBT

- solution focused brief therapy (SFBT)

- dialectical behaviour therapy (DBT)

- narrative therapy

- externalization

- psychoeducation.

I [Fiona] don't use any of the aforementioned in their purest forms but rather the parts of them that fit the individual's needs.

Further options

It can also be useful to use the following, sometimes as standalone interventions and sometimes in conjunction with the above:

- Comic strips.

- Social Stories™.

- Timetabling in many forms, including advice on how to use the virtual assistant 'Alexa'. This supports scaffolding for difficulties with executive functioning.

- Videos and YouTube clips, which sometimes help to consolidate conversations about particular difficulties and demonstrate alignment with other individuals experiencing the same difficulties. Sometimes I use motivators (e.g. anime and Minecraft™) to encourage and enable engagement in interventions.

- Texts and messaging, even when the young people are in the room with me. Sometimes my young people struggle so much with anxiety and social phobia that they find it hard to speak, so this can aid communication and assist with the building blocks of the therapeutic relationship.

- Encouraging and incorporating yogic breathing and exercise in sessions, including mini-assault courses (for the younger ones) or walks/dog walks around the locality near our CAMHS base.

- Cognitive assessment information informs and enhances how you deliver an intervention in order to match the learning style and motivation of the individual. I individualize all my interventions.

- Exercise can be part of the intervention in young people with eating disorders and autism once they have achieved a better-nourished state.

- Fitness tracking devices can be used during exercise and breathing to provide concrete evidence of what happens to the body during exertion or at times of heightened anxiety. They can also demonstrate how it is possible to control the emotional state by managing the physical state. You can use this information to help the young person manage anxiety through exercise and breathing as part of a toolkit of strategies.

SUPPORTING COMMUNICATION

NIAMH

The following is something Niamh and I [Fiona] worked on to support Niamh's transition to college. The words have been made into laminated cards for Niamh to hand to tutors, so that they have informed, individual information. This is an example of how far Niamh has come with her understanding of herself, her ability to communicate this to others, and her understanding of the importance for her and them to share this information. This is not something I would recommend for everyone, but for Niamh it was appropriate and another step in her ladder of communicating effectively with others.

I am Niamh

- I am autistic.

- I have difficulties with communicating.

- I may say things that sound rude but I don't mean them.

- I might not understand what is being said to me. I will try to ask for clarification.

- I might need to have things explained to me in different ways or repeated, or have more support.

- I might be loud when I need to be quiet.

- If I'm inappropriate, please tell me 'That's a bit harsh' or 'Nip it in the bud' or 'Quieten down, Niamh'.

- I might have difficulty to keep up and I want you to know that I am trying and I will always work hard.

- I do tire easily and get stressed easily.

- In general I can get overwhelmed.

- If I'm feeling overwhelmed I might need to:

  - Leave (to be alone). Most of the time I will return but when I return please do not ask me any questions, just carry on. Any fuss or attention makes it worse and may lead to me needing to leave again.

  - If I need to leave college altogether, I will let someone know.

  - If I am too overwhelmed to tell someone at the time, I will go straight home and then either I or my mum will ring college to let you know I am safe.

EATING DISORDERS
Family therapy

Family therapy is the evidence-based treatment for young people with AN and BN (NICE 2017), utilizing the family as a resource in overcoming the young person's illness and achieving a re-nourished state. Family therapy may also be an option for those with OSFED, as the eating disorder may closely resemble features of AN or BN. I often see the family take a defensive position when, as a team, we mention 'family therapy'; however, its purpose is never blaming and its role is more to help families break cycles where the family have become organized around the illness.

It is important to frame family-based treatment (FBT) as the means by which we support parents/carers to support their child or young person to eat. This is because the eating disorder not only affects the child/young person; it also causes a strong ripple effect for those around them.

It is beyond the scope of this book to cover the various components of family therapy for eating disorders; however, approaches have been manualized and are available to review (see Eisler *et al.* 2016; Lock and Le Grange 2015). I [Sharleen] often find that an effective approach is an eating disorder team that will use the principles of these manuals to guide their practice but will be flexible in their approach in achieving the necessary healthy state for each individual they encounter. This is especially true and necessary when working with young people with both autism and eating disorders. For example, concepts such as parents/carers taking 'full control' of all meals provided (first stage of FBT) may actually make things worse, and introducing approaches such as externalization of the illness (seeing the illness as a separate entity, which was borrowed from narrative therapy) may be effective for parents/carers but not for young people with autism themselves.

NICE (2017) indicates that if FBT is 'unacceptable, contraindicated or ineffective', then there are two other approaches to choose from: CBT and adolescent-focused therapy. These are described a little later in this chapter.

REFLECTIONS ON FAMILY THERAPY

HEIDI

Sam, a family therapist, describes his work with Heidi and her parents:

Heidi's parents were surprised when family therapy was offered to them as a treatment for the eating disorder. They had come to the first assessment hoping it would lead to their daughter being seen by someone who would talk to her on her own and help her get over the problem. For me this was an opportunity to explore the different ways Heidi and her parents understood the difficulties and how each of them had different ways of responding to each other. Heidi's parents were of the opinion that much of what they did or said usually had the outcome of either making things worse or making no difference at all for Heidi, which created strong feelings of powerlessness and guilt. Heidi was aware of her parents' frustration, and to avoid further tension she chose to keep her worries to herself.

Heidi wanted her parents to stay with her when she came to appointments, as this made her feel more comfortable. Heidi wasn't confident speaking to others and appreciated how her parents could help to put feelings and events that were hard for her to describe into words, especially as it took Heidi a long time to get used to new people before she felt able to trust them. Early conversations focused on the understanding and impact of the diagnosis, and Heidi and her parents often wondered how they might have caused the illness. Heidi's parents often talked about situations they believed they had not handled very well and the guilt they experienced for not spotting the illness sooner. The conversations provided the opportunity to consider the effect the illness had on their interactions over time and how it might have done this by creating emotional distance between them through tension and arguments, which meant they were unable to talk to each other in ways which left them with feelings of safety and understanding.

Sam describes how being more flexible within his sessions led to a common understanding for both Heidi and her parents in how to communicate to each other:

During the appointments Heidi and her parents listened to each other's worries. Heidi's parents spoke about how it had been helpful for them to come to the appointments, as they had found out things they didn't know about their daughter and what she had been going through. This helped them to speak to her differently and step in when they noticed she was struggling, whereas in the past they had either said the wrong thing (which led to an argument) or had just not known what to do about it and probably picked the wrong time to ask her how she was feeling.

NIAMH

Niamh's mum, Mandy, describes how the strategy of naming Niamh's illness 'Mario', in an effort to see the problem as separate from Niamh, did not work for Niamh:

The advice from CAMHS was to take away Niamh's control over her eating. They gave me some instructions, but when I did this, she got worse. She became more anxious and distressed. We were focusing on getting rid of Mario, her name for her eating disorder and getting Niamh back... I joined forums and groups online to read about others' experiences. They all sounded similar to mine. The school of thought amongst those parents/carers is that eating disorders are not about control or about the child's life experiences – they are a monster living inside them and can happen to anyone, like other illnesses such as cancer. This made sense to me; Mario was our monster. On reflection, however, I don't think this was helpful to us. For Niamh, control was a big part of her eating disorder and her experiences up to that point were definitely relevant... It felt like there was a one-size-fits-all approach for dealing with girls with anorexia and it didn't work for Niamh. She never really engaged with Mario, saying, 'It's me, it's not Mario, it's just me.'

Cognitive behavioural therapy (CBT)

CBT is a therapeutic approach that can help individuals with eating disorders understand the interaction between their thoughts, feelings and eating behaviours, and develop strategies to change unhelpful thoughts and behaviours in order to improve mood and functioning. CBT can be offered on either a self-help or an individual basis. Most of the research on the effectiveness of CBT in eating disorders has been in the adult population, so it is not a recommended first-line treatment in young people with eating disorders such as AN and BN. It is, however, the preferred first-line treatment for adults and young people with BED.

REFLECTIONS ON CBT

HEIDI

Heidi engaged and responded well to CBT, but this was after she had established re-nourishment and it was addressing her depression, low self-esteem and anxiety rather than her eating disorder.

Heidi liked its logical approach and practical application as this fitted with how she liked to process information. Because Heidi was referred to the autism pathway at this stage, the CBT therapist also adapted her practice to meet the needs of Heidi – being matter-of-fact, collaborative and incorporating relaxation and mindfulness techniques within sessions in order to provide Heidi time to process the information. That said, I [Sharleen] have often observed CBT not working with young people with eating disorders and autism; therefore, it is important to consider thinking styles and emotional literacy when considering therapeutic intervention for this cohort of young people.

Adolescent-focused therapy (AFT)

AFT is an individual psychotherapy for young people with AN. It focuses on the young person's ability to change their behaviours, with a supporting role from the therapist and the family. The fundamental view of the approach is that adolescents with anorexia do not feel sufficiently competent or successful in managing the social, personal, familial and developmental challenges of adolescence. They use self-starvation, obsessive thinking and restricting behaviours to manage these anxieties and fears. Through the relationship with the therapist and with the support of parents/carers, AFT aims to help the adolescent safely explore these anxieties, test and challenge them, and learn new skills to build self-confidence and self-esteem.

I [Sharleen] have not personally witnessed or encountered AFT in practice; however, its principles may be an advantageous aspect when working with those with autism and eating disorders; an area, in my opinion, for possible future research.

Practical interventions

Therapy modalities provide structure and meaning to sessions and this often reduces practitioners' anxieties. However, we must not take away the ability to provide practical suggestions that help with daily difficulties and break obsessional cycles. For example, the following suggestions have been useful for those with autism and eating disorders:

- *Distraction techniques before, during and after meals:* These may involve watching television, doing schoolwork, tapping, etc.

- *Soothe box:* This is a collection of, or reminder of, items that are meaningful or helpful, and which may soothe all the senses. These might include a photo album, perfume and a soft blanket.

- *Activities that keep hands busy:* Sewing, knitting, colouring-in, puzzles, for example, can help with restlessness and agitation.

REFLECTIONS ON PRACTICAL INTERVENTIONS

RUTH

Ruth shares with us some strategies which were helpful to her:

- With numbers in terms of exercise I found removing all tracking devices helpful.

- DBT was helpful for emotional regulation. Using a workbook was effective, I think, *but getting to the root cause needs to be looked at.*

- I find mindful photography helps with controlling my emotions; it can slow the explosion down and be quite satisfying. I'll often be distressed and walking too fast and taking my phone out to capture the details of things helps.

- Planning out my free time takes away some of the time from the time thinking about the eating disorder, a really rigid alternative structure.

NUTRITIONAL/DIETETIC INTERVENTION AND STRATEGIES

It is recommended that dietary advice is part of the treatment package for young people with eating disorders (NICE 2017), but the guidance does not indicate who specifically should be giving this advice. Of course, my professional bias means that I [Sharleen] recommend that a registered dietitian fulfils this role. I am highly aware that some family therapy models are structured so that dietetic input is minimal (that is, to provide a structured meal plan only) and a dietitian's direct involvement with the young person or their family is considered unnecessary (Eisler *et al.* 2016). I understand why this position is taken – eating disorders are complex mental health conditions and are not about food *per se*. However, an appropriately trained dietitian can be a powerful resource in the treatment model, going beyond the role of 'meal plan provider' by providing motivational work and nutritional education, being a secure base for families when nutritional queries arise, and being in a unique position to bridge the gap between physical and mental health (O'Connor 2019).

When managing both autism and eating disorders, it is important that the dietitians are flexible in their approach, whilst also being aware of the nutritional aspects of autism – the individual's sensory needs, the differing relationship with food that may have been present prior to the eating disorder, and approaches that are utilized to introduce dietary change.

Dietary preferences

REFLECTIONS ON DIETARY CHANGES

RUTH

Ruth comments on having a dietitian who understood her sensory needs and pre eating disorder food preferences:

> She was able to understand what was eating disorder-related and

what was a historic or sensory issue and adapt accordingly. Previous dietitians had been completely inflexible, which made things more difficult.

NIAMH

You may have noted in Chapter 2 that Niamh made the decision to become vegan. Young people with eating disorders often state a preference to be vegan or vegetarian; however, because of the restrictive nature of these diets, this is often contraindicated until there is significant cognitive and physical restoration. I [Sharleen] explored this choice with Niamh and – in what felt like 'going against the norm' in eating disorder dietetic treatment – I supported her decision to do so as along as she met her nutritional needs to become physically well. Whilst under the eating disorder team, Niamh's rules around food constantly changed and it was often hard to keep track of and manage these. However, I knew that it was important for Niamh that I was led by her. This resulted in Niamh becoming physically healthy (albeit through a limited variety of foods) and her menses resumed.

HEIDI

With Heidi, time was important. Our relationship had been strained since the time on the paediatric ward when her nasogastric tube was passed; therefore, when she was discharged from the SEDU, I [Sharleen] was used on a consultative basis via the family therapist with whom Heidi had a good relationship. After approximately 6 weeks, it was agreed with Heidi that I would join family sessions so that she could refamiliarize herself with me. This meant that I was available for Heidi should she have questions and/or need clarification regarding nutrition (we would have 'toolbox talks' – time-limited information on aspects of nutrition, research and media, alongside written information), but I did not lead in the sessions – my role was largely 'sitting on the bench'. Heidi eventually developed trust in me and was able to see me individually and discuss her relationship with food more openly, sharing that food made her feel very full and that this led to her feeling sick. She reported that this had led to vomiting but that it was involuntary and not self-induced. She expressed frustration that others did not believe she was not 'making herself sick'.

Heidi eventually expressed a wish to transition to solids, but in order to do this she wanted to have only foods that she felt she was comfortable with and ready for. She wanted to work backwards in terms of her 'food' timeline (starting with food she ate prior to her restriction), and to eat at certain times of the day; she also wanted to calorie count so that she knew she was having enough every day. I agreed. If you work in eating disorders, then you will know how this goes against everything you read or learn in this field. I felt seriously uncomfortable about this, but Heidi's presentation was now in the context of autism and that made me stop and change course. Both Heidi and I were going to practise being 'comfortable with the uncomfortable', for very different reasons.

Transitioning to solids was difficult for Heidi from a sensory perspective. She knew she needed to engage in 'mechanical eating' (eating because you have to, not because you want to) in the initial stages, but she found it hugely distressing. However, through collaborative working with both Heidi and her parents, we were able to find a means that dampened this distress, that is by soothing her other senses when she reached feelings of fullness. We had already established that Heidi was very visual and liked sounds that were repetitive in nature. Therefore, we developed flashcards on 'reasons to recover' and made a list of YouTube videos/soundbites, such as tapping and knocking, alongside the relaxed breathing that the CBT therapist recommended. Heidi's transition and increased food intake was gradual. This is what worked for Heidi; however, each plan needs to be individualized and established collectively with the young person and their family.

Other methods to help change food preferences

Other methods have been cited in the literature. The ones that I [Sharleen] utilize or amend within my own practice are:

- *Behavioural experiments:* Testing hypotheses regarding the young people's beliefs around food.

- *Food chaining:* Considering current preferences, where the goal is to link foods that are already eaten with new foods that are similar in taste or texture.

- *Social Stories™ and comic strip conversations:* These are often used with young children but can be useful with older children, too – they can also be the artist.

- *Mindfulness:* This is used to engage the senses with regard to food as well as hunger and fullness.

- *Desensitization and the use of 'taste trials':* This involves spending time around the rejected food with a view to eventually tasting it.

- *Art:* Drawing food groups and/or creating a food collage (helps with desensitization).

Alternative feeding and hydration

I [Sharleen] always advocate eating food as a first-line strategy to achieve re-nourishment, but there are times when other means of feeding need to be considered. In order of preference these are as follows.

1. Oral nutritional supplements (ONS)

ONS are used routinely in paediatric and inpatient eating disorder settings. When food is refused at a meal or snack, then an equivalent measure of ONS is provided. ONS preparations are milk- or juice-based, although only the former (being nutritionally complete) are used in clinical settings. Personally, I [Sharleen] rarely recommend ONS in the community. When I do, it is usually as a last resort (it is difficult for families to manage the ratio of volume of ONS required in lieu of food eaten) as a top-up (the young person will already be on a significant meal plan), or when, like Heidi, the individual has been discharged on ONS from an inpatient setting.

Tolerating liquid may be more acceptable from a sensory perspective as the volume is often a lot less than the food equivalent (this was the reason for Heidi remaining on a liquid diet post-discharge from the inpatient setting).

2. Nasogastric (NG) feeding

As already mentioned, NG feeding is an artificial means of refeeding. A tube is placed through the nose and into the stomach, with nursing staff administering nutritional supplements via a syringe at mealtimes. NG feeding occurs in the hospital setting only for those with eating disorders. During my career as an eating disorder dietitian, the number of times we have made the decision to pass an NG tube has been minimal. It is an option that is chosen only when oral routes of feeding (as already discussed) have been exhausted. Because of its invasive nature, it is never an easy decision to make, and ethically that decision needs to be robust. I [Sharleen] am also aware that it compromises my therapeutic relationship with these young people, but I am willing to temporarily be the 'bad cop' if it means saving their life. Covering all legal and ethical considerations with this treatment method is beyond the scope of this book, but the following is a summary of what I explore before I agree to the insertion of an NG tube:

- Have all other methods been trialled and unsuccessful (within a time frame that has not compromised physical health)?

- Is physical health being compromised because of the lack of nutrition?

- What is the young person's level of motivation and their level of insight into their illness?

- Have the family and young person been made aware of what NG feeding is, the procedure, the pros and cons, and the reasons why it is required in this instance?

- Have the young person or their parents/carers given consent?

- Are the paediatric and eating disorder teams all in agreement?

For those with autism, the passing of an NG tube can be hugely distressing, especially if there are sensory considerations. Indeed, for Heidi it caused a rupture in our relationship. It is always a team decision to pass an NG tube, but because of the nature of what we are trying to achieve the dietitian is often seen as the clinician responsible for making that decision. It is important to reflect every time we decide to pass an NG tube; and as caseloads including those with autism increase, it is necessary to search for ways to quickly reach them so that NG feeding is not needed. I always strive to find alternatives to NG feeding, but compromised physical health is always the deciding factor (i.e. if at that time, NG feeding is in the best interests of the young person). Ultimately, the answer to preventing the necessity for this invasive intervention is the early identification of both autism and eating difficulties.

Autism and diet

Although not within the remit of this book, it is important to consider the increasing popularity of 'special diets' and vitamins as a therapeutic approach in autism. Despite their increasing use, there is a lack of consistent and large-sample, good-quality evidence to support recommendations in their use as a 'treatment' for autism symptoms. The following are a few of the most common dietary 'treatments', for which there is peer-reviewed research available:

- gluten-free casein-free (GFCF)

- exclusion of phenolic compounds and foods high in salicylates

- exclusion of food additives

- yeast-free diet

- oral nutritional supplements

- fish oils and other supplements rich in omega 3 fats

- probiotics and enzymes.

It is important to be mindful that pursuing 'restrictive' diets in those who already have food limitations can be detrimental to their physical and mental health and can further increase their risk of developing an eating disorder.

What is often forgotten when working with young people in general is establishing basic needs, such as the environment, how information is shared and understood, and ensuring follow-through. In most cases, these aspects will not require a lot of adjustment by the practitioner; however, for those with autism, a collaborative approach and possibly a different style of working is required.

REFLECTIONS ON AUTISM AND DIETARY SUPPORT

HEIDI

For Heidi, talking about nutritional information did not help – she found the amount of information overwhelming. In response to this I provided only short nutritional education sessions and gave her more in-depth written information. Heidi found the latter was more useful as it was a secure source that she could refer back to when she was struggling with her anxieties around food.

RUTH

Ruth provides further insight into other ways teams can be flexible in their work with our young people:

Following difficulties with community treatment, I started seeing the manager of the community team. I felt she understood and respected my diagnosis of autism and made adjustments accordingly:

- We met in a quieter location.

- She sent me written summaries.

- She mostly stuck to what she had agreed to do (when she didn't, it was distressing).

- When I reached a stage where I was failing to gain weight and felt stuck, she suggested an admission, but immediately said it would be planned, she would help me to understand everything and we would work on adjustments together.

Hospitalization and inpatient treatment

It's important to address the issue of admission to inpatient. With the government's investment in CYP CEDS, there is a leaning towards care being provided in the community, as the evidence suggests that this is where it is most effective and cost-efficient. This has already led to an observed reduction in specialist eating disorder inpatient beds, which in turn has led to alternative ways of working, such as collaboration with medical paediatric wards as outlined below.

Paediatric admission

Often, medical inpatient units were unable to manage those with eating disorders. They tended to stabilize the patients' physical health and then quickly pass them on to mental health units – a 'stop gap'. However, there has been a shift nationally, where some paediatric medical units have collaborated with the CEDS in developing a pathway of intervention that may range from a few days to 4 weeks. In this model, parents/carers are involved and supported on the ward so that as soon as their son/daughter has physically stabilized they are able to resume care at home. For Heidi, the paediatric ward facilitated physical stabilization, but because of presenting co-morbidities it was not feasible or safe to return Heidi home and a specialist bed was required. That said, I [Sharleen] continually experience the benefits of a collaborative approach on the paediatric ward: I am able to build a therapeutic relationship, observe eating behaviours and liaise with nursing staff regarding various dietary needs – an especially valuable resource when autism is present or suspected.

Specialized eating disorder units (SEDUs)

SEDUs are specialist inpatient units that specifically treat eating disorders. Their interventions and routines differ significantly, and for our individuals with a dual diagnosis of autism and eating disorders there initially needs to be careful consideration regarding the suitability of an admission. If it is deemed necessary by a Care Education Treatment Review (CETRs are for young people who have been or are about to be admitted to a specialist mental health/ learning disability hospital either within the NHS or within the independent sector), then the admission needs to be individualized and planned. Visiting a ward or having a welcome pack prior to admission can help young people become familiar with the new environment. If admissions are not carefully planned so that both autism and eating disorders can be appropriately managed on the ward, the experience can prove to be difficult and overwhelming. However, if autism has not yet been identified in the young person, it is difficult to make adjustments.

REFLECTIONS ON INPATIENT ADMISSION

HEIDI

In Heidi's case, her time on the inpatient unit meant that she was unable to transition to solids – although her sensory needs played a role, we must acknowledge that the environment itself may have hindered her progress.

RUTH

Ruth shares her difficult feelings during one of her admissions:

On admission I was completely overwhelmed. What went wrong?

- Seen by multiple professionals over a short period of time.

- No gentle introduction to the environment – I'd never been there before.

- Noise on the ward. My room was placed opposite the office, and the person in the room next to me was constantly running their taps.

- As a result of the above I shut down. I refused to eat or drink and said I couldn't do this in the unit.

- My blood sugar dropped so low I was moved to the medical ward for treatment. On that ward it was less hectic/noisy. I was able to eat and drink with 1-to-1 support and was discharged from the ward (and my section) after a week. I was still very underweight and unwell. The support I received in the community following discharge was infrequent.

Ruth describes how on another occasion she was supported with adjustments that were made for her planned admission:

- I was given written information about the ward.

- It was agreed I would have orientation visits to the ward prior to admission, being slowly shown around, having a drink in the dining room, meeting members of staff.

- We agreed an admission date.

- I was given information about visiting times and how I could make my room feel more welcoming.

- It was agreed I could have a family member stay with me for the admission process.

- We talked about how time outside was really important to me and agreed that if I was progressing well with the plan, they would look at getting me time off the ward a.s.a.p. even if that involved just sitting on a bench outside.

- They acknowledged my difficulties with noise and agreed they would try and place me in a quiet room away from the office. If this wasn't possible straight away, they would look to move me as soon as someone left. They agreed they would try to let me know where my room would be in advance.

- It was agreed that if I was overwhelmed, I could have my post-meal observations in my room, with the door open for staff to occasionally check. This would only be allowed if I was complying with the programme.

Hospitalization, whether it be on a medical paediatric ward or a specialized inpatient unit, is often not adapted to meet the needs of those with autism and eating disorders. Although there is a strict routine in terms of meals and snack provision, providing much-needed structure, there still remains a lot of uncertainty. This is difficult for any young person with an eating disorder, but especially so for those with co-occurring autism.

Ruth shares aspects of her admission process that she found unhelpful:

- Having said my admission date was 100% definite in a pre-admission appointment, mid-way through, they told me the date had changed. This induced a complete meltdown. I attended the appointment alone – I had no one I knew with me to calm me down. I ended up in the road and was sectioned by the police. My admission took place 2 weeks later. When they gave me the original date, I told them how difficult I'd find it if it changed and they assured me it wouldn't.

- Loud radio in dining room.

- Our places at the table were moved around every week. I found this really difficult, especially as what time they would change things around varied, so I often wouldn't find out until just before a mealtime.

- No introductions of new patients – they were just placed at the table. Not told when someone was moving into room next to mine.

- Temperature of the ward. Often new patients would arrive feeling the cold and would dress inappropriately in thin items of clothing. The heaters would then be put on, which would cause me to overheat and feel distressed.

- I was in hospital over the Christmas period. All groups were cancelled over the Xmas period. When I asked for a timetable of what would be happening, they kept putting off producing one. When one was finally produced, there were question marks next to lots of activities and most things didn't happen.

- No prior notice was often given in respect of changes. I found it easier to cope if notice was given.

- The temperature of my food was often cold. After it caused distress a number of times, they had to produce a care plan for it to be heated up. I've always liked my food to be hot (pre eating disorder). Staff made me feel embarrassed by making an issue out of this.

- Agency members of staff not aware of ward routines; often late to prepare mealtimes, for example getting the items out for snack time should happen 10 minutes beforehand. I would arrive 10 minutes beforehand, so I could prepare mine before it got busy. Sometimes they wouldn't be there until 1 minute before.

- Getting into a routine of having certain accompaniments to meals (e.g. a particular type of fruit), then struggling to cope when that item wasn't there. Pre eating disorder I would often stick to the same foods, so having different things was really difficult (e.g. if I had a pear every day and pears ran out, I'd find it hard to cope).

- Attending groups could be difficult for me. I was allowed to leave groups if it became too much. I found it difficult not to criticize when groups were poorly run/organized and I didn't feel they were therapeutic.

Considering the adaptations required when working with young people with autism in an eating disorder unit may ensure engagement in treatment and improved relationships, which in turn may improve outcomes.

Ruth has kindly shared what helped during her admission:

- The initial assessments during my admission were split up with breaks in-between. The doctor who I saw kept touch to a minimum, explained everything he was doing and gave me the option to stop if anything felt too uncomfortable or difficult.

- On my first day on the ward having staff show me the routines before everyone else came into the dining room. I made sure that I was always on time to mealtimes after that as there was lots to prep which became overwhelming when there were lots of people all trying to do the same thing at once. This could be an important adjustment for someone with autism as the distress caused during food preparation could impact on ability to complete the meal.

- Each day a patient was allocated to a member of staff for support. I found it hard to approach staff and found if easier if they approached me to offer some time.

- I agreed early on that my family would take me off the ward for my leave. I found it too difficult to approach staff to ask them to take me on leave. It would cause distress as they would be unable to give a time, or they would give a time and would change it.

- Being given written information and an agenda for key-work sessions. Writing any 'homework' or agreements down during key-work session. Having a clear written plan for leave and reviewing it afterwards.

- Being allocated to a key-worker who had experience of working with patients with a diagnosis of autism. I had this for my first admission, but for the second I didn't and I didn't feel understood by the person I saw.

- My care co-ordinator came in to visit in the first week and took me off the ward for our appointment, which helped as I was feeling overwhelmed.

- Staff facilitating distractions at the table. I found it hard to initiate conversations with others but having simple word games or quiz questions helped to break the ice.

- Having as few people in ward round as possible. Writing written comments beforehand and giving them to consultant to read.

It is important that we listen to and cater for the needs of young people with autism as they often know what helps them self-regulate.

Here, Ruth shares the personal strategies she used to make things easier whilst an inpatient:

- I used a printed timetable to structure my day outside of groups and mealtimes. I like to have a bath and was able to have one at the same time every evening.

- I requested that I was given a time/day for when I was seeing my key-worker.

- I took things in to make myself feel more at home – soft duvet cover, photos, own mug and tea/coffee.

- I took in headphones to wear.

- I included sitting in the garden in my routine. I would often do this after groups and would listen to music through my headphones to help me to decompress.

- My family downloading things to my laptop to watch so I could stick to my routine of watching certain programmes.

- Family members were allowed to visit during observation times, providing the visit was in my room – this helped.

- Completed an autism passport from the National Autistic Society to give to the ward.

- Had some 'therapy' putty to use at the table. I would also have liked to have a book but this wasn't allowed. Other patients were allowed puzzle books, which caused me frustration as I felt this was 'against the rules'. I also found it hard not to say something when patients were breaking the rules (this is a common feature of autism). Whilst on the ward, I felt I had to adhere to the rules and couldn't understand when others didn't do the same.

Mental Health Act
We do not wish to discuss the use of the Mental Health Act (1983) in detail; suffice to say, it is important to be aware that it is used in those who have impaired insight with regard to their difficulties.

Usually, it is in an eating disorders capacity around food restriction that the Mental Health Act is considered.

Day-patient treatment

Day-patient treatment is eating disorder care that offers mealtime support and therapeutic intervention; the person then returns home each evening. However, there is limited evidence of its efficacy and, as a result, there are very few facilities that offer this approach.

REFLECTIONS ON DAY-PATIENT TREATMENT

RUTH

Ruth shares her views on day-patient treatment:

> Not working and having lots of time alone is really difficult. In an ideal world I would have stepped down into day-patient treatment, but we don't have this in our area. Day-patient treatment in my view would always be more successful for someone on the autistic spectrum. The difficulties around being in close proximity to others can impact on ability to engage in treatment. On both my admissions I discharged myself early without completing the treatment as I found the environment too difficult.

MEDICATIONS

Medication should not be offered as the only treatment for eating disorders (NICE 2017), and therapeutic intervention should be tried across the spectrum of mental health conditions prior to their consideration. The most commonly used medications are antidepressants or selective serotonin reuptake inhibitors (SSRIs), such as fluoxetine and sertraline. It is important that prescribing and monitoring of medication is done under a psychiatrist who specializes in child and adolescent mental health.

It is also important to assess young people's perceptions of what medication will do, as often practitioners believe that medication is refused because of the possible side effect of weight gain, whereas it may be sensory-specific for those with autism.

REFLECTIONS ON MEDICATION

HEIDI

Heidi had been reluctant to start medication which might help the anxiety and low mood, as she had never liked the idea of taking tablets for anything, even if she had a headache. During the assessment, Heidi said she was worried about what a tablet would do inside her, moving her hands towards her stomach as she tried to put her experience into words. She brought her hands close together over her stomach and squeezed them into two tight fists (like a tablet), before opening up both hands at the same time so that her fingers stretched forward and spread out in front of her, moving away from her body like a mini explosion. Heidi's worry was not about weight or shape but about what would happen if she introduced something unknown and unfamiliar to her body. Heidi was therefore started on fluoxetine *in liquid form*, whilst under the eating disorder team.

NIAMH

Niamh was not prescribed any medication whilst under the eating disorder team but currently takes sertraline. Niamh worked hard therapeutically for years with clinicians but had eventually come to a point where her anxiety was not allowing her to move forward with more in-depth work. Again, after much discussion with Niamh, her mum and the MDT, it was agreed to refer Niamh to psychiatry for an assessment, with a view to a possible trial of medication to ease her anxiety and to support further meaningful therapeutic interventions.

JAKE

Jake had had many years of trying to work with clinicians and teachers on the things that he was finding difficult. Eventually, after much deliberation, discussion and collaboration, he was put on medication.

His mother, Samantha, explains:

> Jake was first trialled on sertraline in 2011: 25 mg initially but then increased to 150 mg. The higher dose had a negative effect on Jake, making him very unsettled and irritable, so the dose was reduced to 50 mg, which helped.

A FINAL REFLECTION ON THE THERAPEUTIC RELATIONSHIP

Ultimately, whilst there are various manualized therapy models with a convincing evidence base in the treatment of mental health conditions in children and young people, the therapeutic relationship is crucial and should not be underestimated. If young people trust you, they will feel safe enough to take risks and experiment with difference, regardless of their presenting illness – something that Mandy (below) explains was an important aspect in her daughter's treatment.

NIAMH

> When Niamh met the psychologist from the eating disorder team, she initially hated her with a passion, but they slowly managed to form a bond. She finally had someone to talk to. She allowed Niamh to take out her frustrations on her and wasn't offended by anything Niamh did or said, and slowly Niamh began to trust her. This, and an appointment with a doctor who told her she might have a heart attack, was the start of her recovery. However, I think that ultimately Niamh started to get physically better because she wanted to. She was tired of being cold and weak and wanted to dance again.
>
> ———— *(Mandy)*

CHAPTER 7

Recovery and Understanding of Self

'I learnt it's ok to be who I am and that it's ok if that is different... that I can still be happy, in myself and in my life and that I'll be ok.'

(*Niamh*)

'Knowing yourself is the beginning of all wisdom.'

(*Aristotle*)

To clarify from the outset, recovery is discussed in the context of the eating disorder and not with regard to autism. Autism is not something one recovers from; it is an inherent part of who these young people are. More importantly, we must support and acknowledge the power of self-understanding and what it brings on a systemic level for every young person – not only those who have autism but also those who don't.

UNDERSTANDING OF SELF – LABELS AND DIAGNOSES

Understanding of self, self-understanding or self-concept is a general term used to refer to how someone thinks about, evaluates or perceives themselves. Bardone et al. (2013) looked specifically at self-concept in eating disorder recovery and found that positive self-concept might help to maintain recovery. Within the clinical field there has been much debate on the use of diagnoses and labels – especially with regards to autism and eating disorders independently

135

– and their effect on the person who is being diagnosed or labelled, and whether it hinders or helps their understanding of self. As clinicians often working in a system that is structured around labels and diagnoses, we need to respect the lived experience and realize that the value of a label and its relationship with self-understanding is very much dependent on the young person in front of us.

WHAT DO WE KNOW ABOUT RECOVERY?

According to the Cambridge Dictionary (https://dictionary.cambridge.org), recovery is:

> the process of becoming well again after an illness or injury; the process of becoming successful or normal again after problems; the process of getting something back.

This definition takes a very simplistic view of recovery, and many would argue it does not hold value in the context of mental health. As indicated in Chapter 1, there has been wide-scale debate on accurately defining recovery within the field of eating disorders, leading to various parameters being used in outcome studies to assess effectiveness of treatment options. As a result, there have been varying rates of recovery ranging from 3% to 96%, depending on the criteria used (Couturier and Lock 2006). Weight and reduced frequency of eating disorder symptomology are often aspects that are easily captured and measured, whereas qualitative data in the form of personal experiences appear more abstract to decipher and categorize. Indeed, even service design and culture can stunt a holistic approach to recovery. Despite this, research is shifting, albeit very slowly, towards capturing 'expert by experience' voices – personal perspectives on a person's illness and recovery.

The 'expert by experience' voice identifies further criteria for recovery which fall under the emotional and psychosocial umbrella (Bjork and Ahlstrom 2009; Dawson, Rhodes and Touyz 2014; Musolino *et al.* 2016) and beyond the medical model definition. Whilst identifying fundamental criteria for eating disorder recovery according to recovered individuals, Alexander de Vos *et al.* (2017) recommended including measurements of psychological well-being, including positive relationships with others, self-acceptance, autonomy, personal growth, social contribution, and self-adaptability in addition to remission of eating disorder symptoms.

Hashtag recovery (#recovery)

It would be naïve of me [Sharleen] to discuss recovery and the lived experience without discussing the role and impact of technology, especially with regards to the influence of social media. The main resource for communication and education amongst young people, social media is an intricate phenomenon of our time that can do both harm and good. As indicated in Chapter 3, the use of social media and online resources should be assessed and continually explored during treatment. Platforms such as Twitter, Instagram and other online forums have been shown to create a sense of community and a shared 'recovery identity' (Chancellor, Mitra and De Choudhury 2016; La Marre and Rice 2017), providing motivation and inspiration for those on their eating disorder journey. The positive effect of such information needs to be balanced with the documented negative impact of conflicting messages – especially where disordered eating and behaviours are disguised as 'recovery'. This can be particularly difficult for those with autism – an aspect that Ruth covers later in this chapter.

REFLECTIONS ON RECOVERY ON SOCIAL MEDIA

NIAMH

By this point [discharge from eating disorder services], Niamh was almost famous within the Instagram eating disorder community. She'd created this whole persona around her anorexia and didn't want to let it go. This was her new passion – she liked being anorexic – she had a focus and an identity that people seemed to like.

(Mandy)

Recovery in those with eating disorders and autism

Because research between eating disorders and autism is in its infancy, there is minimal literature on recovery in this sub-group of the population. What evidence there is suggests that there is longer illness duration, higher illness severity and poorer responses to treatment with AN compared with individuals without autism (Nielsen *et al.* 2015). A clinical case study of two children with co-morbid AN and autism suggested that the rigidity and low introspection characteristic of autism hindered responses to traditional therapeutic strategies (Doudova, Kocourkova and Koutek 2015). This implies that adapted or targeted treatments are required in order to establish 'recovery' in these individuals.

The lived experience evidence base

The 'expert by experience' is a means by which we can learn about achieving recovery through appropriate intervention in those who have experienced, or continue to experience, eating disorders in the autism community. Unfortunately, as it stands, there is no research that explores these lived experiences.

Establishing the young person's perspective and exploring the underlying drivers in maintaining the eating disorder in those with autism may lead to different responses and alternative ways of working. Baron-Cohen *et al.* (2013) also called for working differently in this cohort of people:

> Clinicians may find it useful to shift the focus of intervention away from the battle over weight and towards helping the patient to recognize that they have a mind that is more attracted to systems and less to people's emotional lives.

Broadening our understanding of obstacles to recovery, especially in those who are portrayed as 'challenging' and 'non-compliant', to a position of people's experiences of self-care and health (Musolino *et al.* 2016) will undoubtedly have a positive effect on the therapeutic relationship and recovery outcomes.

REFLECTIONS ON THE RECOVERY PROCESS

RUTH

Ruth shares aspects of her daily living that 'get in the way' of her 'recovery':

- Keeping my scales and continuing to weigh myself – this continues to fuel my eating disorder.

- Continuing to track my walking steps (I did sell my fitness tracker but I downloaded another one).

- The sensory feelings of gaining weight. I struggle with the feeling of weight gain on my skin.

- The physical side effects of eating more. I struggle with health anxiety. Throughout being unwell with an eating disorder I have always read information about eating disorders, so when I get side effects from eating more, I panic and fall back into bad routines and behaviours.

- Dealing with my emotions – the eating disorder had dampened my mood swings.

- The routines of the eating disorder are so well established it's hard not to fall back into them. I moved into my house whilst unwell and I associate a lot of the routines with my home.

- Unhelpful things can become a special interest for those who are autistic. I have read a huge amount of information around eating disorders, including lots of information online. Social media helped to fuel my eating disorder and taught me things I wouldn't have thought of myself. The thirst for knowledge and information can be used in the wrong way in terms of eating disorders and I think professionals need to be better at asking people about their social media usage (and forums) as this can help maintain eating disorders (I've never once been asked about my internet usage).

- Not working and having lots of time alone is really difficult.

HEIDI

You may remember that Heidi found calorie counting soothing. For her, the process of counting reduced her anxiety. She responded to written information, and through this she recognized that she needed to make changes. She made the shift to increase her calories but continued to count them as she found this soothing. Using this system, recovery looked different for Heidi: she was able to stay physically well, she was able to increase the variety of food she would eat, and she gained a deeper understanding of herself. Although behaviours that we often associate with an eating disorder remained, such as calorie counting and rigid timings of meals (that is not to say that Heidi will not address these things in the future), there was better understanding of the purpose behind these behaviours and they no longer impacted on Heidi's daily functioning.

NIAMH

Mandy shares how obstacles with eating are still around for Niamh, but there is a greater understanding:

> She still needs encouragement to have a varied diet. She'll still say, 'Tell me what to have for breakfast', but then be furious if I don't say the thing she wanted. She still finds making those choices for herself hard. She'll still say, 'I don't know why but I feel a need to only eat healthy things.' With encouragement she can eat anything, but I worry about the future.
>
> Fiona has encouraged Niamh to embrace her difference and she has started to do that. The language she uses about herself has become more positive. She still struggles with her feelings, as she always has, and still says she doesn't know what normal is, but I feel that her diagnosis has given her a better sense of self, an identity.
>
> I think that the eating disorder was a way to have some control in a world that felt so alien to her. I also think she felt so little of herself that she just wanted to disappear. I think she was physically and emotionally tired from masking all day and was initially so anxious that she couldn't eat and it then became her new obsession.

LIVED EXPERIENCE REFLECTIONS ON RECOVERY AND UNDERSTANDING OF SELF

NIAMH

Fiona asked me how I felt about the diagnosis, I think everyone expected me to be upset but I wasn't upset at all. Being diagnosed with autism felt like a relief in a way. It explained a lot about myself and a lot about what had happened to me. I started to learn more about myself, how I could help myself. I realized it was ok to be overwhelmed and that I could cope on my own. I became more comfortable with who I am. Eventually I have ended up confident in myself.

——— *(Niamh)*

Niamh has embraced her diagnosis and has gradually started to understand and manage her feelings and, for the first time I think, to really get to grips with her relationships with others. Niamh is still very rigid in her thinking with regards to other people – she either likes them or she doesn't. This can be their voice, their face or general personality but I have noticed that she is learning to stop and think about the reasons for this and she is sometimes able to show empathy and understanding. She will still say that she doesn't like someone's face but says that they can't help it and at least she should be nice.

When things are difficult, Niamh will say, 'I'll speak to Fiona about this', and banks it for the next session. I honestly live in fear that this will end – I know we only have a year at the most left in children's services and it scares the life out of me.

I feel that Niamh's understanding of herself and the way she fits into the world is only just beginning. She struggled to see the impact of her behaviour on others and I think the most change has come from the fact that Niamh is beginning to like herself. But also because as a family we have tried to understand Niamh more in the context of her autism and we have adapted our day-to-day lives accordingly. Niamh used to say that she couldn't wait to leave home and have her own life, which was sometimes upsetting for me to hear, but I think that she actually just wants to have some control over who she sees, where she goes and what she does. We have more order in our lives generally and it has helped massively. Now that I know what she needs, we talk carefully about what might happen in advance and what we will do if something changes. Looking back, I think Niamh did a lot of things to please me. I am quite a sociable person and so is her older brother, and I think she thought that was non-negotiable.

Now she has two close friends and she is happy with that. She has been able to speak to them about her difficulties and they understand she may need time alone. They have an agreement that Niamh can say if she needs them to leave and they are not offended by this, as so many of her friends have been in the past. Her circle is small but strong. Niamh is preparing for college in September, her first time back in the education system in five years. I do worry as eating seems to still be her go-to thing to control when her anxiety is high. Things are so much better but not perfect.

(Mandy)

Years later my husband saved me from a life of eating disorder by simply sharing his love of food and confidence in eating. His mission in life, simply because he loves and cares for me, was to take me out for meals to feed me up and make me stronger. This was eventually consolidated by my autism diagnosis, which enabled me to begin to understand what autism is and how it colours my perspective on life.

(Kay)

The thing that's helped me most is having a bit of self-awareness, and that's not really come from services, that has come from my own research and my own, just, everyday living through it and starting to be able to recognize patterns and behaviours. So, the self-awareness is quite important. My family have been helpful, obviously. They're there day-to-day, so they're living through it with me. Unfortunately at the moment, as I said before, it's really hard getting the right kind of support. So, for about seven years now, I go through a cycle of becoming unwell, which often leads to all my other mental illnesses getting worse, which often leads to then having to go into hospital, and then coming out and not getting the right support, and then the whole cycle starts again. It's a very complex issue and I think we need to be doing the research to be able to build this model of what AN, or anorexia nervosa, looks like in autistic women, to be able to kind of adapt treatments and approaches that are available.

(Elliott and Mandy 2018)

How autism causes or affects eating disorders, I do not know. But for me, it is a way to cope with a world that scares me. It is a way to keep connected to my body when sensory issues make me want to tear my skin off. Autistic people can become fixated on certain facts, numbers, and patterns. I am fixated on a specific weight and every day begins either happy, because I am below it, or miserable and full of anxiety because I am over it. Black-and-white thinking makes food good or bad and dress sizes acceptable or not acceptable.

(Beckwith-Fellows 2017)

OUR REFLECTIONS ON RECOVERY IN PRACTICE

FIONA

'Recovery' is not something that has ever entered into my vocabulary in relation to my work within autism, because autism is not something to recover from. However, for those individuals having to manage their eating challenges every day, I understand why recovery is important and necessary.

The main themes that have stood out for me from the words and experiences of the individuals in this book, which appear to have had a significant impact on their everyday functioning and well-being, are:

- family
- love
- understanding of self
- self-acceptance
- good nutrition

- exercise

- doing more of the things they love to do

- limiting stress in their lives

- the recognition of patterns of behaviours

- the right services at the right time

- self-management of the impact of sensory processing and integration

- understanding and self-management of concrete thinking

- understanding and management of anxiety and emotional regulation

- ritualistic thoughts and behaviours

- understanding of the young people as individuals and understanding of the conditions from others: people close to them, clinicians and professionals, services and the wider community.

SHARLEEN

I am a strong believer in recovery and I am highly aware that it looks different for each individual who enters our service – an aspect that, for me, took time to appreciate. I entered the field of eating disorders with strong views on what recovery was, and I strived and fought every inch of the way (my dogged 'fix it' mentality shining through) for young people to achieve this. The result was a very emotionally tired and exhausted young patient and me.

Keski-Rahkonen and Tozzi (2005) found that views on recovery changed according to the sufferer's current stage of change, and I believe this is an important consideration. I have learned a lot from the young people I work with. I have learned to sit with them in the current place that they are, what that looks like and how it feels: is it different from a week ago? How does it compare with the life before the illness? What does it means for their future? I am there to instil hope and to give a 'nudge' when they struggle by themselves.

When I first encountered young people with restrictive eating and autism, I had to reconsider my position on recovery yet again. Indeed, I could get them to a place of nourishment through adapting my practice but I had to acknowledge that traits of obsessionality and rigidity were a part of who they were, and that we both needed to work within these realms – understanding the traits and their purpose, recognizing when the traits were negatively impacting on health, and utilizing those very same traits to achieve a place of safety instead.

Just like the means by which it is achieved, there is no 'one size fits all' in recovery for those who have experienced eating disorders amongst the autism community. Recovery is fluid; shifting and moving in response to the environment around them. For some people, eating disorder thoughts and cognitions no longer play a role in their life; for others, they reappear at times of stress. Although research is seeking means to capture all pillars of recovery, we as practitioners need to respond to the individual (and families) in front of us, be open to different ways of working, and acknowledge their inner and outer world in order to achieve their recovery. For this to occur, we require a service and culture change that supports such flexible working and thinking.

CHAPTER 8

Service and Culture Change

We feel constantly torn between being extremely proud to be a nurse and a dietitian in specialist services working with, on the whole, phenomenal clinicians, who are not only empathic and knowledgeable but hardworking and resilient, whilst feeling saddened and astonished that there is still so much more that needs to be done to support our young people. We remain bewildered that there is still so much stigma and misunderstanding and lack of knowledge around difference.

In an era where diversity and being an individual and embracing difference are promoted everywhere we turn, one would hope that as much passion and commitment would be invested into timely, appropriate, quality services for people with autism and eating disorders.

You have read and heard the voices of individuals speaking to you throughout this book. They repeatedly refer to the need for:

- more specialist training for educators, social care, the medical profession, the nursing profession and society as a whole

- more specialist clinicians working in generic areas

- more resources for community services

- a change in inpatient clinical interventions and service delivery

- consistency of care

- joint working

- increased understanding and awareness of autism and eating disorders

- improvements in communication between professionals and services

- more collaboration with 'experts from experience'

- specialist but holistic care.

When we tell people about the clinical areas that we work in, we are often met with 'That must be tough?', 'How do you do it?', 'I could never do that!' Conditions and illnesses that are outside of people's radars and understanding become a foreign entity to them – they focus on the perceived difficulty of that condition/illness and not on the human being and their family that sit in front of us. Unfortunately, these questions not only come from the general public but from the health care practitioners around us. This is a hugely sad state of affairs, but we also understand their position. It is not easy to work in the unknown, with no evidence base or guideline directing our practice, no safety, no security. This is the very place that these young people with autism find themselves in every day because they are trying to fit into a societally constructed box labelled 'normal'. We owe it to these young people to venture into their unknown place, to be curious and to work towards a system that works around them instead of the other way around. The shift in understanding and service provision is colossal but not impossible.

Mair Elliott shares her experience and reflection of services when having both autism and an eating disorder:

> I think, from a personal experience, I've had extreme difficulty getting the right support, and I still haven't to this day, so I still get into loops of restrictive eating and becoming very unwell, because when I access the standard treatments and approaches that are available on the National Health Service, they're all focused around body image and body weight, and that's not the primary concern from my perspective in terms of my food problems. And so, what often happened is that I will start accessing some kind of support, it

won't be relevant or appropriate to what I'm experiencing, I tend to feel like I'm not being listened to, and I also get accused of choosing to not engage, and then they withdraw the support, which then is a very frustrating situation to be in, especially when every time I've fallen unwell, I actually am asking for help, but that relevant or appropriate support isn't available. And also, professionals just don't have the awareness or the knowledge of what it is to have comorbid ASD with mental illness and anorexia nervosa, and they don't understand the interplay between the two diagnoses and what that can mean for someone living with the two diagnoses. It's very, very hard, currently, if you're in this situation that I am in, to get the appropriate support. (Elliott and Mandy 2018)

SERVICE DELIVERY AND PROFESSIONAL KNOWLEDGE

At present, eating disorder services are commissioned and resourced to see eating disorders that are outlined in the NICE guidelines (NICE 2017); however, this has highlighted service gaps and ethical dilemmas. Because eating disorders is a specialist service based on a very structured and manualized approach, people often forget that other specialist knowledge and provision are required to support it. As societal culture around us changes significantly, it would be naïve of the systems and their practitioners to assume that eating disorder presentation would not alter in response. This is becoming very apparent in the service that we work in, with an increasing number of young people presenting to the eating disorder services who are later identified as having autism. Unfortunately, eating disorder clinicians often feel out of their depth in managing this cohort of young people as they do not have the skills to do so.

REFLECTIONS ON WHAT NEEDS TO CHANGE

JAKE

Samantha (Jake's mum) says:

What would I change?

- Schools' understanding of ASC and children's individual needs.

- All the staff involved with Jake in the early years were amazing and very passionate about their roles in young people's lives. All it takes is just one doctor not to listen or do what's in the young person's best interests and that can cause a lifetime of damage.

- The need for better communication between professionals/ parents/carers and to have time to talk away from the young person.

- It's important to listen to the young person, as if they do not feel comfortable with the professional, they will not talk or listen; instead they will shut down.

- As adults we can choose to ask for a second opinion; children should have this option, too.

- The transition from children's services to adult services is shocking.

RUTH

Ruth observes:

More training is needed regarding medical monitoring. Often the GP surgery would ask me as the patient what I was there to have monitored. Crisis and community mental health team need training, specifically how to manage an eating disorder-related crisis, as often eating disorder services are only 9 to 5 weekdays.

Point of access

There is no standardized eligibility criteria in CAMHS. Each team interprets information differently, depending on who screens and what their own knowledge, experience and belief systems are. For example, some clinicians feel that it is unfair to put children in 'diagnostic' boxes, so they push against eligibility criteria. Sometimes this comes from their clinical background and sometimes it is because they know there are limited services to address the particular needs they are screening. However, if you do not have robust eligibility criteria and do not stick to them, you run the risk of not highlighting service deficiency to commissioners, so you end up putting sticking plasters over the problem. The result of this is overstretched, under-resourced teams lacking in specialisms, and long waiting lists (and when you get to see a clinician, they may not be the most appropriate to address your individual need).

If GPs, schools and generic referrers are not well informed on clinical presentations (e.g. girls presenting with potential autistic traits or boys with susceptibility to eating disorders), then their referrals will not reflect their actual need. The consequence of this will be a rejected referral or inappropriate services.

Crisis management

Training and increased knowledge on both autism and eating disorders for those who regularly encounter these young people (outside of the eating disorder services) would greatly enhance efficacy of care, especially those in crisis management services (GP, A&E, paramedics, out-of-hours mental health teams). These are often the points where young people enter the service, and although they are often anxiety-provoking and fast-paced environments, the first impression needs to be holistic and patient-centred. For those who are already known to services, it is important that there is a collaborative approach to intervention and support. It also has to be said that if we can effectively identify autism earlier, then we may have a reduction in those presenting in crisis in their later years.

So, we come back full circle to the need for training. The training needs to be targeted at primary care services, schools, medical and nursing training facilities, education facilities, the police, social care, universities and colleges, parents/carers and the young people themselves. The right people need to be listened to, included and consulted, to influence and implement change. We can help to influence the educators and consult with others outside of our services, and we can also actively implement change within our own services.

Education and training – what does it look like?

Education and training – or to coin the term used in the clinical field, 'continuing professional development' (CPD) – is central to how we continue to manage and interpret the world around us in each of our respective fields. As much as emerging research and evidence-based guidelines should be core to this training, those experts from lived experience also need to be integral to our understanding.

University teaching

Recruiting practitioners to the fields of autism and eating disorders is, and always has been, difficult. They are subject areas that are skimmed over, if not completely ignored, at university level, and are deemed 'specialist', something 'you can learn later' within the health care professions. We need to provide spaces that allow practitioners (students or otherwise) to be curious and supported, by building foundations within the university education system. Examples are:

- Clinician- and 'lived experience'-led lectures/seminars.

- Integrating mental health into all health, education and social care discipline courses.

- Student health care placements to include specialist areas such as eating disorders and autism.

- Language around nutrition and the influence of their own belief systems.

- Understanding of emotional processing, literacy, flexible versus inflexible thinking, and theory of mind – these are vital in establishing the therapeutic relationship.

- Einstein famously said, 'The more I learn, the more I realize how much I don't know.' We must include 'what we don't yet know' and how we explore this as part of our conversation as practising clinicians. From personal experience, university teaching consists of 'this is everything you need to know about this illness' (which is undeniably important) and 'this is how we "fix" it', with often evidence-based guidelines as the place of safety. Autism and eating disorders are clinical areas where there is little evidence base (which we explore later in the chapter), so we need to feel confident navigating this 'unknowing'.

Empowering professionals

Taking a position of curiosity is difficult: venturing into that unknown space can feel hugely uncomfortable for both the professional and the young person. However, we must support professionals and clinicians to take this critical step, providing them with education and knowledge, as well as giving them appropriate access to supervision and training. Systems that encounter children and young people on a daily basis (schools, medics, health and social services) need to be trained in:

- identifying autistic traits

- how they differ in the male and female population

- what to do when they suspect autism

- how their practice may need to adapt in response to that – approach, communication style and environment

- early signs of eating difficulties and obsessionality around food and the context behind them

- physical health implications of malnutrition

- diet culture (see page 155).

For this to occur, systems need to be supported in having regular access to those who have experience in these fields. We are great believers in 'knowledge is power'; however, we need to make sure that the system supports this attainment of knowledge. For eating disorder services, having established and timetabled team consultations and supervision space with an experienced ASC practitioner should be an essential part of the multi-disciplinary model.

Assessment and therapy modalities

We don't have the answer on what the 'perfect' assessment looks like and we don't think there is an answer, as that is very much dependent on the young person in front of us. As practitioners, we need to have additional resources within our assessment toolkit to enhance the journey for the young person and also to lay the foundations for that all-important therapeutic relationship. This is of benefit not only to us as practitioners but to the system as a whole.

We understand the need for therapeutic pathways and the offer of manualized therapeutic packages – they provide structure and direction. We are not suggesting that this should necessarily change, but it's important to consider flexible approaches and moulding them to the needs of the young person. This may require practitioners using their knowledge in a more creative and explorative way, as we have discussed throughout the course of this book. It also requires the system to support this level of flexibility, such as looking at the spaces in which we see people, commissioning cross-pollination of specialist services instead of their being separate entities, and involving young people and their families in every aspect of these aforementioned pathways.

RESEARCH

Eating disorders and autism both together and independently have, in recent times, received a lot of media attention; however, the space they occupy within the research world is small compared with other clinical areas. Disparity in funding allocation has been observed within eating disorders and autism, taking up a small proportion of already poorly funded mental health research. This makes it difficult to enhance our knowledge in the respective areas. On the clinical floor, we often discuss the importance of parity of esteem between physical and mental health, and this viewpoint should also be allied to funding research.

We must also be mindful that gender bias exists in our research knowledge of these conditions, with females dominating the eating disorder data and males being the predominant presentation in autism data. This is not necessarily intentional, but altering the focus through a different gender lens may produce a more systemic understanding of these conditions, which may subsequently lead to earlier identification and intervention.

If we examine the direction of the research that has been completed, there has been a bias towards the underlying science of the conditions (i.e. the biological and genetic aspects) instead of lived experiences, aspects of recovery and alternative interventions that may be deemed to be of more practical value. This undoubtedly limits the therapeutic landscape when we try to manage these conditions not only independently but also when they co-occur. We acknowledge that there is more research under way on the relationship between eating disorders and autism than ever before, but we are mindful that, like this book, it has leaned towards those with restrictive eating practices. It is important that, with the same level of open mindedness and curiosity, we explore autism in the context of other eating disorders. Understandably, research is often carried out and completed by academics, but it is vital that we utilize and support clinicians to shape and carry out future directions in research.

A NOTE ON DIET CULTURE

Diet culture is everywhere and it can be exceptionally difficult to navigate what is real and reliable and what is just another money-making scheme that is taking advantage of people's vulnerabilities. Frustratingly, diet culture even seeps through the veins of the health, education and social care systems, that is, the people within it, their own beliefs and the language that they use around food. They are not to blame – telling fact from fiction in nutrition, especially online, is a difficult trick to master. But, imagine what this must feel like for someone who has autism. Diet culture is not going to disappear overnight, but we can teach our future generation how to find a way through it in the following ways:

- We can be mindful of our language around food (e.g. by not labelling food as 'good' or 'bad').

- We can have conversations about how people come in all shapes and sizes.

- We can be social media literate – always taking a curious position about what we read and see online.

- We can acknowledge our own belief system around nutrition and weight (e.g. where it has come from) before imparting nutritional knowledge to others.

We will forever strive for a system that embraces all kinds of differences. We make it our fight each and every single day and we do this for the remarkable and incredible young people we encounter. And we owe it to those young people and their families to never give up.

A FINAL REFLECTION

NIAMH

Here are some final words from Niamh's mum, Mandy:

> There are so many layers to this so I think that an earlier diagnosis would have made those years so much easier for Niamh to cope with. I feel sad that Niamh has spent so much of her life confused and not understood by the people around her – especially me.

Final Words

We met as a direct result of an office refurbishment and the need to share a small space – prior to this we did not know of each other's existence! We were aware of each other's disciplines but distanced ourselves from venturing into the other's world as we believed that it was neither necessary nor applicable to our own work. On reflection, it was likely that we just didn't want to see what we actually now see so clearly: we felt powerless when faced with the unfamiliar. This changed. 'Corridor conversations' evolved into multi-disciplinary consultations and subsequent joint sessions. Increased knowledge and confidence gained by talking to each other improved our willingness to work differently with this amazing group of young people. Eating disorder services are confined by eligibility that is underpinned by diagnostic criteria – criteria that are limiting when we see a need that cannot be met elsewhere. Specialist services need to be able to look holistically at the young person and be able to reach out to other specialist services to support the young person with autism. For this to happen, we need to know that each other exists, we need to be willing to share, to educate and to empower – the very skills we utilize with our young people.

We do not claim to be experts in autism and eating disorders; we are still learning from our young people, and this means a constant evolution and evaluation of our own practice. However, we are now more open to stepping into the unknown and we want others to explore this space also. This book provides the foundations to unearthing that curiosity.

When it comes to working with young people with eating disorder and autism – think differently!

Fiona and Sharleen

References

Abrahams, B.S. and Geschwind, D.H. (2008) 'Advances in autism genetics: On the threshold of a new neurobiology.' *Nature Reviews Genetics 9*, 5, 341–355.

Alexander de Vos, J., LaMarre, A., Radstaak, M., Ariane Bijkerk, C., Bohlmeijer, E.T. and Westerhof, G.J. (2017) 'Identifying fundamental criteria for eating disorder recovery: A systematic review and qualitative meta-analysis.' *Journal of Eating Disorders 5*, 34. DOI: 10.1186/s40337-017-0164-0.

American Psychiatric Association (2000) *Diagnostic and Statistical Manual of Mental Disorders (4th edition) (DSM-IV).* Washington, DC: American Psychiatric Association Publishing.

American Psychiatric Association (2013) *Diagnostic and Statistical Manual of Mental Disorders (5th edition) (DSM-5).* Washington, DC: American Psychiatric Association Publishing.

Arcelus, J., Mitchell, A.J., Wales, J. and Nielsen, S. (2011) 'Mortality rates in patients with anorexia nervosa and other eating disorders: A meta-analysis of 36 studies.' *Archives of General Psychiatry 68*, 7, 724–731.

Asperger, H. (1944) 'Die "Autistischen Psychopathen" im Kindesalter [Autistic psychopaths in childhood].' *Archiv für Psychiatrie und Nervenkrankheiten 117*, 76–136.

Attwood, T., Garnett, M.S. and Rynkiewicz, A. (2011) *Questionnaire for Autism Spectrum Conditions (Q-ASC).* Accessed at https://www.ncbi.nlm.nih.gov/pubmed/29052806 on 09/03/2020.

Bardone, A.M., Schaefer, L.M., Maldonado, C.R., Fitzsimmon, E.E. *et al.* (2013) 'Aspects of self-concept and eating disorder recovery: What does the sense of self look like when an individual recovers from an eating disorder?' *Journal of Social and Clinical Psychology 29*, 7, 821–846.

Baron-Cohen, S., Jaffa, T., Davies, S., Auyeung, B., Allison, C. and Wheelwright, S. (2013) 'Do girls with anorexia nervosa have elevated autistic traits?' *Molecular Autism 4*, 1, 24.

Baron-Cohen, S., Leslie, A.M. and Frith, U. (1985) 'Does the autistic child have a theory of mind?' *Cognition 21*, 1, 37–46.

BEAT (2015) *The Costs of Eating Disorders – Social, Health and Economic Impacts.* Accessed at www.beateatingdisorders.org.uk/uploads/documents/2017/10/the-costs-of-eating-disorders-final-original.pdf on 25/04/2019.

Beckwith-Fellows, C. (2017) *I Have an Eating Disorder Because I'm Autistic.* National Association Eating Disorders Blog.

Belmonte, M.K., Allen, G., Beckel-Mitchener, A., Boulanger, L.M., Carper, R.A. and Webb, S.J. (2004) 'Autism and abnormal development of brain connectivity.' *Journal of Neuroscience 24*, 42, 9228–9231. DOI: 10.1523/JNEUROSCI.3340-04.2004.

Berument, S.K., Rutter, M., Lord, C., Pickles, A. and Bailey, A. (1999) 'Autism screening questionnaire: Diagnostic validity.' *British Journal of Psychiatry 175*, 444–451.

Bjork, T. and Ahlstrom, C. (2008) 'The patient's perception of having recovered from an eating disorder.' *Health Care for Women International 29*, 8, 296–944.

Bleuler, E. (1908) 'The Prognosis of Dementia Praecox. The Group of Schizophrenias.' In J. Cutting and M. Shepherd (eds) (1987) *The Clinical Roots of the Schizophrenia Concept: Translations of Seminal European Contributions on Schizophrenia*. Cambridge: CUP Archive.

Bould, H., De Stavola, B., Lewis, G. and Nadia Micali, N. (2018) 'Do disordered eating behaviours in girls vary by school characteristics? A UK cohort study.' *European Child and Adolescent Psychiatry 27*, 11, 1473–1481.

Brugha, T., Cooper, S.A., McManus, S., Purdon, S. *et al.* (2012a) *Estimating the Prevalence of Autism Spectrum Conditions in Adults: Extending the 2007 Adult Psychiatric Morbidity Survey*. Leeds: NHS Information Centre for Health and Social Care. Accessed at https://pdfs.semanticscholar.org/efe8/77ab95ca23b45c6aa72c77ea643e67f23a08.pdf on 09/12/2019.

Brugha, T., McManus, S., Smith, J., Scott, F. *et al.* (2012b) 'Validating two survey methods for identifying cases of autism spectrum disorder among adults in the community.' *Psychological Medicine 42*, 3, 647–656.

Buckholdt, K.E., Parra, G.R., Anestis, M.D., Lavender, J.M. *et al.* (2015) 'Emotion regulation difficulties and maladaptive behaviors: Examination of deliberate self-harm, disordered eating, and substance misuse in two samples.' *Cognitive Therapy and Research 39*, 140–152.

Chancellor, S., Mitra, T. and De Choudhury, M. (2016) 'Recovery amid pro-anorexia: Analysis of recovery in social media.' *Proceedings of the SIGCHI Conference in Computing System*, 2111–2123. New York, NY: ACM.

Couturier J. and Lock, J. (2006) 'What is recovery in adolescents' anorexia nervosa?' *International Journal of Eating Disorders 39*, 7, 550–555.

Currenti, S.A. (2010) 'Understanding and determining the etiology of autism.' *Cellular and Molecular Biology 30*, 2, 161–171 .

Currin, L., Schmidt, U., Treasure, J. and Jick, H. (2005) 'Time trends in eating disorder incidence.' *British Journal of Psychiatry 186*, 132–135.

Davies, H., Schmidt, U., Stahl, D. and Tchanturia, K. (2011) 'Evoked facial emotional expression and emotional experience in people with anorexia nervosa.' *International Journal of Eating Disorders 44*, 6, 531–539.

Dawson, L., Rhodes, P. and Touyz, S. (2014) '"Doing the impossible": The process of recovery from chronic anorexia nervosa.' *Qualitative Health Research 24*, 4, 494–505.

Doudova, L., Kocourkova, J. and Koutek, J. (2015) 'Early-onset anorexia nervosa in girls with Asperger syndrome.' *Neuropsychiatric Disease and Treatment 11*, 1639–1643.

Duerden, E.G., Oatley, H.K., Mak-Fan, K.M., McGrath, P.A. (2012) 'Risk factors associated with self-injurious behaviors in children and adolescents with autism spectrum disorders.' *Journal of Autism and Developmental Disorders 42*, 11, 1495–1498.

Durkin, M.S., Maenner, M.J., Newschaffer, C.J., Lee, L.-C. *et al.* (2008) 'Advanced parental age and the risk of autism spectrum disorder.' *American Journal of Epidemiology 168*, 11, 1268–1276.

Ehlers, S. and Gillberg, C. (1993) 'The epidemiology of Asperger syndrome: A total population study.' *Journal of Child Psychology and Psychiatry 34*, 8, 1327–1350.

Eisler, I., Simic, M., Blessitt, E., Dodge, L. *et al.* (2016) *Maudsley Service Manual for Child and Adolescent Eating Disorders.* South London and Maudsley NHS Foundation Trust – King's Health Partners. Accessed at www.national.slam. nhs.uk/wp-content/uploads/2011/11/Maudsley-Service-Manual-for-Child-and-Adolescent-Eating-Disorders-July-2016.pdf on 01/09/2019.

Elliott, M. and Mandy, W. (2018) *Transcription of Interview on Anorexia Nervosa in Autistic People with Mair Elliott and Dr William Mandy.* Accessed at https:// network.autism.org.uk/sites/default/files/ckfinder/files/Transcription%20of%20 Mair%20Elliott%20and%20Dr%20William%20Mandy.pdf on 12/08/2019.

Elsabbagh, M. and Johnson, M.H. (2010) 'Getting answers from babies about autism.' *Trends in Cognitive Science 14*, 2, 81–87.

Fairburn, C.G. and Beglin, S. (2008) 'Eating Disorder Examination Questionnaire.' In C.G. Fairburn (ed.) *Cognitive Behavior Therapy and Eating Disorders.* New York, NY: Guilford Press.

Fairburn, C.G. and Bohn, K. (2005) 'Eating disorder NOS (EDNOS): An example of the troublesome "not otherwise specified" (NOS) category in DSM-IV.' *Behavioral Research Therapy 43*, 6, 691–701.

Fairburn, C.G. and Harrison, P.J. (2003) 'Eating disorders.' *Lancet 361*, 9355, 407–416.

Fardouly, J. and Vartanian, L.R. (2015) 'Negative comparisons about one's appearance mediate the relationship between Facebook usage and body image concerns.' *Body Image 12*, 82–88.

Field, A.E., Sonnenville, K., Micali, N., Crosby, R.D. *et al.* (2012) 'Common eating disorders predictive of adverse outcomes are missed by the DSM-IV and DSM-5 classifications.' *Paediatrics 130*, 2, e289–e295.

Fisher Bullivant, F. (2018) *Working with Girls and Young Women on the Autism Spectrum: A Clinician's Guide.* London: Jessica Kingsley Publishers.

Fombonne, E. (2009) 'Epidemiology of pervasive developmental disorders.' *Pediatric Research 65*, 6, 591–598.

Gauvin, L., Steiger, H. and Brodeur, J.M. (2008) 'Eating-disorder symptoms and syndromes in a sample of urban-dwelling Canadian women: Contributions toward a population health perspective.' *International Journal of Eating Disorders 42*, 2, 158–165.

Grandin, T. and Scariano, M. (1986) *Emergence: Labeled Autistic.* Novato, CA: Arena Press.

Hay P. (1998) 'The epidemiology of eating disorder behaviors: An Australian community-based survey.' *International Journal of Eating Disorders 23*, 4, 371–382.

Johnstone, Ll. (2012) 'Formulation: The psychological alternative to diagnosis.' *Clinical Psychology and People.* Accessed at https://clinpsychthinking.wordpress. com/2012/11/25/formulation-the-psychological-alternative-to-diagnosis on 21/11/18.

Kalm, L.M. and Semba, R.D. (2005) 'They starved so that others be better fed: Remembering Ancel Keys and the Minnesota Experiment.' *The Journal of Nutrition 135*, 6, 1347–1352.

Kanner, L. (1943) 'Autistic disturbances of affective contact.' *Nervous Child 2*, 217–250

Keski-Rahkonen, A., Hoek, H.W., Susser, E.S., Linnia, M.S. *et al.* (2007) 'Epidemiology and course of anorexia nervosa in the community.' *American Journal of Psychiatry 164*, 8, 1259–1265.

Keski-Rahkonen, A. and Tozzi, F. (2005) 'The process of recovery in eating disorder sufferers' own words: An internet based study.' *International Journal of Eating Disorders 37*, Suppl. S80–86.

Kinnaird, E., Norton, C. and Tchanturia, K. (2017) 'Clinicians' view on working with anorexia nervosa and autism spectrum disorder comorbidity: A qualitative study.' *BMC Psychiatry 17*, 292.

LaMarre, A. and Rice, C. (2017) 'Hashtag recovery: #eating disorder recovery on Instagram.' *Social Sciences 6*, 3, 68.

Lavender, J.M., De Young, K.P. and Anderson, D.A. (2010) 'The Eating Disorder Examination Questionnaire (EDE-Q): Norms for undergraduate men.' *Eating Behaviors 11*, 119–121.

LaVigna, G.W. and Willis, T.J. (1995) *Challenging Behaviour: A Model of Breaking the Barriers to Social and Community Integration*. Los Angeles, CA: Institute for Applied Behavioral Analysis.

Lock, J. and Le Grange, D. (2015) *Treatment Manual for Anorexia Nervosa 2nd Edition: A Family Based Approach*. New York, NY: Guilford Press.

Lotter, V. (1966) 'Epidemiology of autistic conditions in young children.' *Social Psychiatry 1*, 3, 124–135.

Machado, P.P.P., Machado, B.C., Gonçalves, S. and Hoek, H.W. (2007) 'The prevalence of eating disorders not otherwise specified.' *International Journal of Eating Disorders 40*, 3, 212–217.

Mandy, W. and Tchanturia, K. (2015) 'Do women with eating disorders who have social and flexibility difficulties really have autism? A case series.' *Molecular Autism 6*, 6. DOI: 10.1186/2040-2392-6-6.

Mansour, S., Rozenbiat, V., Fuller-Tyszkiewicz, M., Paganini, C., Treasure, J. and Krug, I. (2016) 'Emotions mediate the relationship between autistic traits and disordered eating: A new autistic-emotional model for eating pathology.' *Psychiatry Research 245*, 119–126.

Mehanna, H.M., Moledina, J. and Travis, J. (2008). 'Refeeding syndrome: What it is, and how to prevent and treat it.' *British Medical Journal 336*, 7659, 1495–1498.

Mental Health Act (1983) London: HMSO. Accessed at www.legislation.gov.uk/ukpga/1983/20/pdfs/ukpga_19830020_en.pdf on 10/08/2019.

Mette Bentz, M.S., Moellegaard Jepsen, J.R., Pedersen, T., Bulik, C.M. *et al.* (2017) 'Impairment of social function in young females with recent-onset anorexia nervosa and recovered individuals.' *Journal of Adolescent Health 60*, 1, 23–32.

Micali, N., Hagberg, K.W., Petersen, I. and Treasure, J.L. (2013) 'The incidence of eating disorders in the UK in 2000–2009: Findings from the General Practice Research Database.' *BMJ Open 3*. Accessed at https://pdfs.semanticscholar.org/cdd6/33a5d2e8620f153eaed77d4e8991a4b86920.pdf?_ga=2.41840866.1310149569.1568994014-443749780.1565269114 on 25/05/2018.

Miller, J.S., Bilder, D., Farley, M., Coon, H. *et al.* (2013) 'Autism spectrum disorder reclassified: A second look at the 1980s Utah/UCLA Autism Epidemiologic Study.' *Journal of Autism and Developmental Disorders 43*, 1, 200–210.

Milton, D.E.M. (2012) *So What Exactly Is Autism?* London: Autism Education Trust Competency Framework for the Department for Education.

Milton, D.E.M. (2014) 'Autistic expertise: A critical reflection on the production of knowledge in autism studies.' *Autism 18*, 7, 794–802.

Musolino, C., Warin, M., Wade, T. and Gilchrist, P. (2016) 'Developing shared understandings of recovery and care: A qualitative study of women with eating disorders who resist therapeutic care.' *Journal of Eating Disorders 4*, 36.

Neumark-Sztainer, D., Wall, M., Larson, N.I., Eisenberg, M.E. and Loth, K. (2011) 'Dieting and disordered eating behaviors from adolescence to young adulthood: Findings from a 10-year longitudinal study.' *Journal of the American Dietetic Association 111*, 7, 1004–1011.

NHS England (2015) *Access and Waiting Time Standard for Children and Young People with an Eating Disorder: Commissioning Guide.* London: National Collaborating Centre for Mental Health: NHS England.

NICE (2017) *The National Institute for Health and Care Excellence.* Accessed at www.nice.org.uk/guidance on 4/08/2019.

Nicely, T., Lane-Loney, S., Masciulli, E., Hollenbeak, C.S. and Ornstein, R.M. (2014) 'Prevalence and characteristics of avoidant/restrictive food intake disorder in a cohort of young patients in day treatment for eating disorders.' *Journal of Eating Disorders 2*, 1, 21.

Nicholls, D. (2012) *CR168. Junior MARSIPAN: Management of Really Sick Patients under 18 with Anorexia Nervosa. Royal College of Psychiatrists.* Accessed at www.rcpsych.ac.uk/docs/default-source/improving-care/better-mh-policy/college-reports/college-report-cr168.pdf?sfvrsn=e38d0c3b_2 on 16/07/2019.

Nielsen, S., Anckarsater, H., Gillberg, C., Gillberg, C., Rastam, M. and Wentz, E. (2015) 'Effects of autism spectrum disorders on outcome in teenage-onset anorexia nervosa evaluated by the Morgan-Russell outcome assessment schedule: A controlled community-based study.' *Molecular Autism 8*, 6, 14.

O'Connor, G. (2019) *Clinical Guidelines for Dietitians Treating Young People with Anorexia Nervosa: Family Focused Approach.* British Dietetic Association. Accessed at www.bda.uk.com/regionsgroups/groups/mentalhealth/groupresources/clinicalguidelinesfortreatingyoungpeoplewithan (restricted access) on 15/04/2019.

Payakachat, N., Tilford, J.M., Kovacs, E. and Kuhlthau, K. (2012) 'Autism spectrum disorders: A review of measures for clinical, health services and cost-effectiveness applications.' *Expert Review of Pharmacoeconomics & Outcomes Research, 12*, 4, 485–503.

Pellicano, L. and Hiller, R. (2013) 'Anorexia and autism: A cautionary note.' *The Psychologist 26*, 780.

Reba-Harreleson, L., Von Holle, A., Hamer, R.M., Swann, R., Reves, M.L. and Bulik, C.M. (2009) 'Patterns and prevalence of disordered eating and weight control behaviors in women ages 25–45.' *Eating and Weight Disorders 14*, 4, e190–e198.

Ro, O., Reas, D.L. and Rosenvinge, J. (2012) 'The impact of age and BMI on Eating Disorder Examination Questionnaire (EDE-Q) scores in a community sample.' *Eating Behaviors 13*, 2, 158–161.

Russell, T.A., Schmidt, U., Doherty, L., Young, V. and Tchanturia, K. (2009) 'Aspects of social cognition in anorexia nervosa: Affective and cognitive theory of mind.' *Psychiatry Research 168*, 3, 181–185.

Russell-Mayhew, S. (2007) 'Preventing a continuum of disordered eating: Going beyond the individual.' *Prevention Researcher 14*, 3, 7–10.

Rutter, M. (2005) 'Aetiology of autism: Findings and questions.' *Journal of Intellectual Disability Research 49*, 4, 231–238.

Rutter, M., Bailey, A. and Lord, C. (2003) *The Social Communication Questionnaire*. Los Angeles, CA: Western Psychological Services.

Sainsbury, C. (2000) *Martian in the Playground: Understanding the Schoolchild with Asperger's Syndrome*. Bristol: Lucky Duck.

Schieve, L.A., Rice, C., Devine, O., Maenner, M.J. *et al.* (2011) 'Have secular changes in perinatal risk factors contributed to the recent autism prevalence increase? Development and application of a mathematical assessment model.' *Annals of Epidemiology, 21,* 12, 930–945.

Schopler, E., Van Bourgondien, M.E., Wellman, G.J. and Love, S.R. (2010) *Childhood Autism Rating Scale (2nd edition)*. Los Angeles, CA: Western Psychological Services.

Schulte-Ruther, M., Mainz, V., Fink, G.R., Herpertz-Dahlmann, B. and Konrad, K. (2012) 'Theory of mind and the brain in anorexia nervosa: Relation to treatment outcome.' *Journal of the American Academy of Child and Adolescent Psychiatry 51,* 8, 832–841.

Shea, E. (2015) *Eating Disorder or Disordered Eating? Eating Patterns in Autism*. Network Autism. Accessed at http:/network.autism.org.uk on 04/04/2019.

Smink, F.R.E., van Hoeken, D. and Hoek, H.W. (2012) 'Epidemiology of eating disorders: Incidence, prevalence and mortality rates.' *Current Psychiatry Reports 14,* 4, 406–414.

Smith, A.R., Hames, J.L. and Joiner, T.E. (2013) 'Status update: Maladaptive Facebook usage predicts increases in body dissatisfaction and bulimic symptoms.' *Journal of Affective Disorders 149,* 1–3, 235–240.

Smith, K.E., Mason, T.B., Murray, S.B., Griffiths, S. *et al.* (2017) 'Male clinical norms and sex differences on the Eating Disorder Inventory (EDI) and Eating Disorder Examination Questionnaire (EDE-Q).' *The International Journal of Eating Disorders 50,* 7, 769–775.

Solmi, F., Hotopf, M., Hatch, S.L., Treasure, J., and Micali, N. (2016) 'Eating disorders in a multi-ethnic inner-city UK sample: Prevalence, comorbidity and service use.' *Social Psychiatry and Psychiatry Epidemiology 51,* 3, 369–381.

Starlight and Stories (2014) 'A blog by a mummy who is also a teacher.' Accessed at https://starlightandstories.com/category/autism on 09/12/2019.

Svirko, E. and Hawton, K. (2007) 'Self-injurious behavior and eating disorders: The extent and nature of the association.' *Suicide and Life-Threatening Behaviour 37,* 409–421.

Sweeting, H., Walker, L., MacLean, A., Patterson, C., Raisanen, U. and Hunt, K. (2015) 'Prevalence of eating disorders in males: A review of rates reported in academic research and UK mass media.' *International Journal of Men's Health 14,* 2.

Syed-Abdul, S., Fernandez-Luque, L., Jian, W., Li, Y.C. *et al.* (2013) 'Misleading health-related information promoted through video-based social media: Anorexia on YouTube.' *Journal of Medical Internet Research 15,* 2, e30.

Tchanturia, K., Happe, F. and Godley, J. (2004) '"Theory of Mind" in anorexia nervosa.' *European Eating Disorders Review 126,* 361–366.

Tchanturia, K., Larsson, E. and Adamson, J. (2016) 'How anorexia nervosa patients with high and low autistic traits respond to group Cognitive Remediation Therapy.' *BMC Psychiatry 16,* 334.

Tchanturia, K., Larsson, E., Adamson, J. and Westwood, H. (2017) 'Autistic traits in anorexia nervosa: A naturalistic study in an inpatient treatment programme.' *Autism 23*, 1. Accessed at https://journals.sagepub.com/doi/full/10.1177/1362 361317722431?url_ver=Z39.88-2003&rfr_id=ori%3Arid%3Acrossref.org&rfr_dat=cr_pub%3Dpubmed on 12/05/2019.

Times, The (2007) 'Is anorexia the female Asperger's?' 17 August 2007. Accessed at www.thetimes.co.uk/article/is-anorexia-the-female-aspergers-80wp5r9ftw6 on 12/04/2019.

Treasure, J. (2013) 'Coherence and other autistic spectrum traits and eating disorders: Building from mechanism to treatment. The Birgit Olsson lecture.' *Nordic Journal of Psychiatry 67*, 1, 38–42.

Treffert, D.A. (1970) 'Epidemiology of infantile autism.' *Archives of General Psychiatry 22*, 431–438.

Van Son, G.E., Van Hoeken, D., Bartelds, A.I, van Furth, E.F. and Hoek, H.W. (2006) 'Time trends in the incidence of eating disorders: A primary care study in the Netherlands.' *International Journal of Eating Disorders 39*, 7, 565–569.

Volkmar, F.R., Klin, A., Siegel, B., Szatmari, P. *et al.* (1994) 'DSM-IV autism/pervasive developmental disorder field trial.' *American Journal of Psychiatry 151*, 1361–1367.

Werling, D. and Geschwind, D. (2013) 'Sex differences in autistic spectrum disorders.' *Current Opinion in Neurology 26*, 2, 146–153.

Westwood, H., Mandy, W. and Tchanturia, K. (2017) 'Clinical evaluation of autistic symptoms in women with anorexia nervosa.' *Molecular Autism 16*, 8, 12.

Westwood, H. and Tchanturia, K. (2017) 'Autism spectrum disorder in anorexia nervosa: An updated literature review.' *Current Psychiatry Reports 19*, 7, 41.

Williams, D. (2002) *Nobody Nowhere: The Extraordinary Autobiography of an Autistic.* New York, NY: Perennial.

Wing, L. (1996) 'Autistic spectrum disorders.' *British Medical Journal 312*, 327–328.

Wing, L. and Gould, J. (1979) 'Severe impairments of social interaction and associated abnormalities in children: Epidemiology and classification.' *Journal of Autism and Developmental Disorders 9*, 11–29. (Available from the NAS Information Centre.)

Wing L, and Potter, D. (2002) 'The epidemiology of autistic spectrum disorders: Is the prevalence rising?' *Mental Retardation and Developmental Disabilities Research Reviews 8*, 3, 151–161.

World Health Organization (2018) *International Classification of Diseases for Mortality and Morbidity Statistics (11th revision) (ICD-11).* Accessed at https://icd.who.int/browse11/l-m/en on 31/07/2019.

Index